Credit Mana
for
Law Firms

Credit Management for Law Firms

Julia Walden
MA, Hons
Head of Credit Control, Lupton Fawcett, Solicitors

CLT Professional Publishing Ltd
A Division of Central Law Group

© Julia Walden and CLT 1999

Published by
CLT Professional Publishing Ltd
A division of Central Law Training Ltd
Wrens Court
52–54 Victoria Road
Sutton Coldfield
Birmingham B72 1SX

ISBN 1 85811 189 7

All rights reserved. No part of this publication may be reproduced, stored in a retrieval system, or transmitted, in any form or by any means, electronic, mechanical, photocopying, recording or otherwise, without the prior permission of the publisher.

The moral right of the author has been asserted.

Typeset by Jane Conway

Printed by Antony Rowe

Dedication

To my Parents and my son Alexander

Contents

Preface ix

Chapters

Part I: The Place of Credit Management in the Firm   1

    Introduction 3
1. Successful Debtor Control and the Client Relationship 9
2. Minimising Financial Exposure 27
3. Maximising the Value of the File 33
4. The Billing Stage 37

Part II: The Credit Management System   51

The Policy
5. Creating the Policy 57

The Procedures 65
6. Selecting Suitable Chasing Procedures 67
7. Exposure Levels 75
8. Setting Up the Administration 81
9. Collection Techniques 95
10. Selection and Training of Personnel 117
11. Tips for the Credit Controller for Basic Problem Avoidance 131

Part III: Reporting   135

12   Debtors Reporting   137
13   Preparation for a Reporting Structure   143
14   The Structure and Formatting of Reports   153
15   Taking a Closer Look at a Debtors Report   163
16   Reports within the Debtors Report   171

Index   185

Preface

Credit Management for Law Firms has been developed in response to the increasing financial and competitive pressures now facing Law Firms.

The legal environment is extremely competitive and legal practices now have to act as any other business. Clients are looking for a quality service – but at a price. In order to be competitive, survive and do better, practices need to ensure that they keep their cash collections at optimum levels. There is a finite amount of work in the market: getting maximum value from your practice's share of that market sector is of paramount importance. All practices should be aware that they are in effect offering their clients unsecured credit facilities.

I must add at this point that the purpose of the *Credit Management for Law Firms* is not to replace the individuality of the reader's practice by text book dogma, but rather to give a set of parameters by which any practice can base its relationship with its client, making the relationship both comfortable and profitable. At the very least, it will provide a benchmark against which to measure what other firms already do.

The evolution of a new payment culture is not an overnight task. Solicitors have to change themselves before they can begin to change their client's behaviour. Achieving this is dependent on both fee earner and support staff – the whole firm working together. The traditional frictions between the finance department and individual fee earners "protecting" their clients are no longer acceptable. CLT have developed a disk to accompany the book (in order that the *whole* firm can be trained) and made available a TEN Video on cash flow to ensure that the message can be got over effectively. The same disk provides precedents so that the firm has ready access to model letters and reports.

Credit Management for Law Firms is the first stage of that evolution.

I would like to thank everyone at Lupton Fawcett for their support during the writing of this book. In particular, special thanks to Kevin Emsley, the Managing Partner at Lupton Fawcett who has nurtured the book through its many stages of development and answered endless questions on good management practice.

Julia Walden, November 1998

Part I

The Place of Credit Management in the Firm

Part I

Introduction

Introduction 4
Team working using a Credit Management System 6

Part I

Introduction

There was a time when the members of the legal profession considered it to be almost unprofessional to discuss with a client how he was going to finance his case. Asking him to pay his bill at the end of the case was certainly not "the done thing". The financial climate of the 1980's and 1990's has meant that to take this attitude is to take great risks. If a practice is to survive it must become financially aware and attuned to the harsh realities of business. Late payment of bills eats into profit margins.

The legal environment is increasingly competitive, with the client placing emphasis on both quality and price. The private client increasingly has the confidence to 'shop around' and the purchase of legal services can even be regarded as no more exceptional than buying a cooker. The commercial client is quite prepared to have his eggs in more than one basket by using several solicitors for different cases. This of course gives the client unprecedented power and ensures that the solicitors used will keep their costs competitive.

In this environment, any practice, irrespective of its client base, has to ensure that it gets maximum value from its market share to maintain its stability and to fund its growth: in short, to guarantee its survival. Those who do not adapt will fall by the wayside. It can no longer be a case of 'don't chase Bert for his bill, he's a friend'.

The evolution of a new way of thinking about debtors will not happen overnight. Each individual practice will have to evaluate where it currently stands and in which direction it wants its credit policies to go. The purpose of this book is to help legal practices evaluate their current position and formulate effective policies and procedures to control, monitor and maximise the profitability of those clients who will become debtors. The guidelines are intended to minimise the unnecessary taxation hearings, costs draftsmen's fees and debt recovery proceedings, all of which reduce the potential profitability of the fee earner's work. Just as seriously, they damage the client relationship and with it the opportunity of further instructions. The policies recommended are not intended to constrain the individuality of each practice or fee earner but rather give guidance for a profitable framework in which the Client/Fee earner relationship can operate comfortably.

Debtor levels not only affect the well being of a practice but act as a marker of its solvency and liquidity. The debtors ledger is often the biggest user of available working capital. It should not be forgotten that bills issued to clients do not represent merely the work of the solicitor. The fees rendered, which are of course usually put in terms of time spent, also a contain an element of other costs to the practice such as heat, light, secretarial support etc. Bills from the suppliers of these services still have to be paid.

Without the conversion of possible profit into actual profit, *i.e.* debtors into cash, the working capital levels will not be replenished and in time will become depleted. This of course means that it will be impossible to take the profits or to re-invest in the practice.

Case 1

Slap Dash & Co has had an excellent year – with 100% of its available fee-earner time chargeable. Overheads are about 60% of chargeable hours. Their clients are paying an average of six months in arrears. The Senior Partner is quite content though, because he can rub his hands and think of the profit.

Slap Dash's "Profit"

	Chargeable Hours%	Overheads%	"Profit"%	Payments%
Quarter 1	100	60	+40	0
Quarter 2	100	60	+40	0
Quarter 3	100	60	+40	100
Quarter 4	100	60	+40	100
		−240	+160	+200

In the year profits have been spectacular, yet expenses are in excess of payments. None of the profits can be realised without borrowing against the future collections. This is expensive.

Also, what happens if the following year Slap Dash hit a recession, or fee-earners leave, pushing chargeable hours down?

6 Credit Management

The Need for Control and Monitoring

To ensure that the debtors ledger realises as much profit as possible, it is necessary for a practice to set up a system of controlling and monitoring the cash flow implications of the three interrelated stages of work flow.

The Three Work Flow Stages

Input Start Client/Practice Relationship

Throughput Work Carried Out On The Client's Behalf

Output Bill Issued By The Practice For Work Done

To achieve this, as part of a credit management system, a financial reporting structure needs to be put in place.

Team working using a Credit Management System

Successful Credit Management is dependent on both fee earner and administration staff working together.

The four cornerstones on which a profitable practice is built, needs the input of both fee earning and administrative staff:

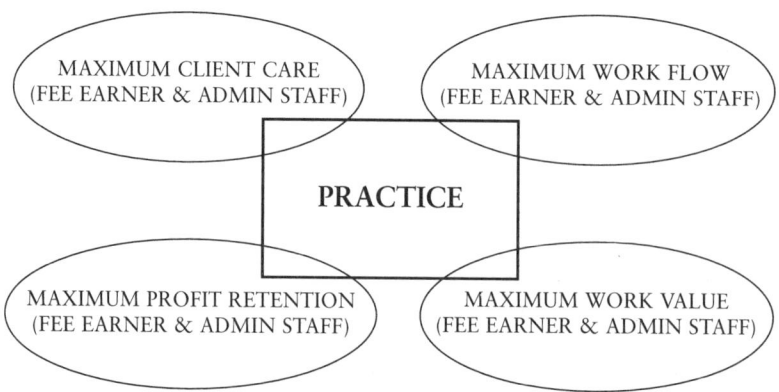

Figure 1: The Four Cornerstones of the Profitable Practice

At any point in the client relationship, both fee earner and administration staff will be in direct or indirect contact with the client. The whole team will be inputting into the relationship: be it the receptionist on his first visit, or subsequent telephone calls to the fee earner's secretary once the work is progressing. That same team can be involved in the accounting process. To ensure maximum value is obtained for the work, the fee earner may send his time sheets and bills to the accounts department for posting. Or the inputting may be done at departmental level by a secretary or in some cases the fee earner himself. Ensuring rapid payment of the bill will be down to both the fee earner in setting up the original client agreement and the credit controller who will chase the bill if it not paid within the practice's specified credit terms. So the invisible barriers between the two, which are often present in legal practices, need to be pulled down.

The setting up of a Credit Management System (*i.e.* a policy *and* a procedure) is one way of establishing a clear understanding of the contribution made to the practice by the operation of both types of staff. The policy should give clear guidance of what is expected of each party, the procedure should guide the individual through the practical steps necessary to adhere to that policy. The basic message should read:

- **Fee Earners need to be released from debt chasing to work on files**
  (which obviously generates further fees).
- **Credit Control staff need to be allowed to get on with collecting debts**
  (Unhindered by requests of special favours for certain clients.)
  And most importantly it should emphasis:
- **The level of debt affects the profitability of the Practice**

In the most basic of terms, ultimately:

No Cash Flow = No Practice

Step by Step

If a practice is able to set up a system to manage, control and monitor work flow, and match it with proactive credit management and reporting, it will improve its cashflow and in doing so increase levels of profitability. The easiest way of doing all of this is to take each step at a time.

The following diagram clearly shows how each step leads onto the next until the practice's optimum profit is achieved.

> Step 1: obtaining a good client relationship – including payment terms
> Step 2: minimisation of financial risk
> Step 3: maximisation of work value
> Step 4 good billing systems
> Step 5: an effective credit control system
> Step 6: good reporting to ensure that all are informed about progress

The end result of all these steps, as long as billing levels themselves are high enough, is a profitable practice, with good client relations.

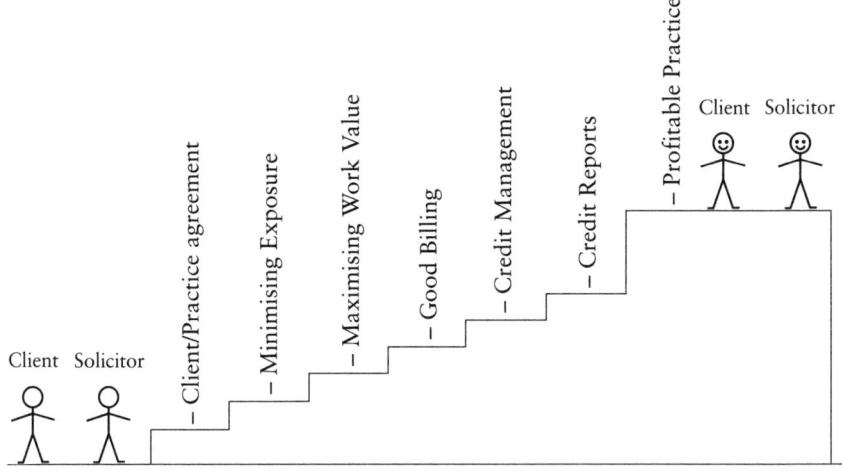

Figure 2: Steps to a Profitable Practice

Chapter 1

Successful Debtor Control and the Client Relationship

Introductory	10
The First Meeting – Laying Your Cards On The Table	11
What The Agenda Should Cover	12
Aspects of the Agenda	14
Has the Aim of the Meeting been Achieved?	18
After the Meeting	18
What if the Client Brings in More Work?	23
Summary	25
Achievements	25

Chapter 1

Successful Debtor Control and the Client Relationship

Introductory

Client: Practice Relationship – A Two Way Street

The client base of a practice is the source of its profit. It is essential therefore that as much as possible is done to nurture that base and ensure that the firm retains as much of its potential profit as possible. Good client management will lead to increased profitability. Client management has to begin as soon as the client is introduced to the practice. From the very beginning the relationship is based on mutual need. The practice needs a client base from which to generate its turnover. The client, on the other hand, needs quality legal services at the right price. Both want payment at the "right" time – the practice as early, and the client as late, as possible.

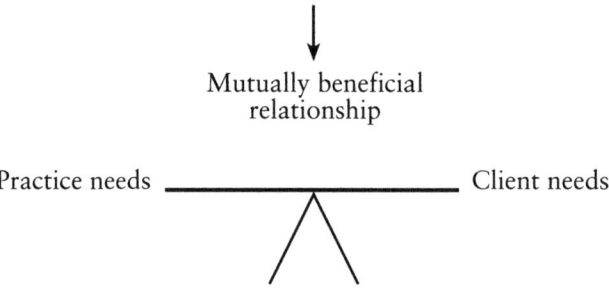

Figure 3: The balancing act

The essential element is to secure a satisfactory method of proceeding for both sides and to this end the fee earner will need all his negotiation skills. If he fails, and gives too much emphasis to the practice's needs, the client will leave without giving the practice the opportunity to provide the service. Alternatively if he gives too much to the client it may cost the practice a percentage of profitability perhaps through disagreement over bills rendered during and at the end of the case. It is essential, therefore, that fee earners understand that the client must be prepared for the financial aspects of the case before he becomes a debtor.

> ### Objectives
>
> In this chapter, it will become clear why it is important that the whole practice:
>
> 1. Knows why it is important to establish the ground rules in the client relationship
> 2. Is able to set an agenda to cover the ground rules at the first client meeting
> 3. Is able to provide a written confirmation of what has been agreed in a form understandable to clients.

The First Meeting – Laying Your Cards On The Table

The first meeting with the client is exceptionally important. Not only is it an opportunity to obtain instructions on one matter, but it should be seen as an opportunity to lay the foundation of a long term relationship with that client. It should be borne in mind that if the client is satisfied and uses the practice over and over again, there is a good chance that he will recommend it to others. This will of course widen the client base of the practice and in doing so increase its potential profitability.

The first meeting is the time when the client decides you are for him: but it also true vice versa. After all there is always the chance that he is not the client for the practice – particularly if payment terms are going to be an issue.

Prior to meeting the client an agenda should be prepared. This should cover the subjects which the fee earner will need to establish with the client. When preparing the agenda the fee earner should bear in mind the client/practice relationship see-saw as pictured above. He should consider the needs of the client and he should consider the needs of the practice. Having the agenda will ensure that the fee earner can focus his mind on this balancing act without being taken off track.

Also important is that at this initial meeting the fee earner is able to establish all the client data he is likely to need, especially to check for any conflict of interests. Finding out several months later that one of the other fee earners is suing the client does not look very professional!

The initial interview: a warning note

It should be made clear to the client (or potential client as he still is at this stage) whether the practice charges for the first interview. This area can cause some confusion as it is by no means across the board that there is no charge for an initial meeting. For example, a person may come to the practice, and then (for whatever reason) decide not to proceed to use the practice or not to proceed with the case at all. If the client gets charged for what they assumed was a free interview, the practice will find it difficult to obtain payment. Sending a client care letter with the bill when no agreement has been made is of no use. The amount of the bill raised for that initial interview will probably prohibit legal action on grounds of expense, and it may damage the reputation of the practice to boot. If a practice is going to charge, it must be made clear to the prospective client before they come in and see a fee earner.

What The Agenda Should Cover

The agenda discussed on the following page is not intended to be definitive, but should be read as a guide as to what could be included for discussion at a first meeting. Each individual practice will need to analyse what it and its clients will require. Obviously the client's needs will be dependent on the type of work undertaken.

A Sample Agenda

1. The Framework of the case
   - The case and how it is to proceed

2. Contact
   - Who will be dealing with the client
   - Who is to be approached in the absence of the fee earner

3. Timetable of the case
   - Are there statutory limits?
   - Has the client a deadline?

4. Responsibility
   - What the client will need to do and what the solicitor undertakes to do

5. Financial aspects of the case
   - Fee levels
   - How it is to be funded
   - The risks undertaken by the client (if relevant)
   - Arrangements for disbursements and billing
   - Estimates of cost

6. Complaints procedures

7. Database details
   - Name
   - Address
   - Work details
   - Phone Numbers

8. Any other business
   - Matters arising from discussion

It is should be borne in mind when preparing the agenda that it is not uncommon for clients to come to the initial meeting distressed, confused and or angry depending on their circumstances. The purchase of legal services often can be a "distress purchase" and so the person conducting the interview has to make every effort to be empathetic with the client, whilst at the same time keeping his eye on the practical matters at hand. The agenda should help the fee earner focus on his objectives and not be swayed by the emotional pleas of the client to such an extent that his judgement becomes clouded.

Aspects of the Agenda

1. Framework of the case

The framework of the case, *i.e.* how it is going to proceed and what is likely to happen, need to be discussed in a way in which the client can understand. The client should be treated with respect. Blinding the client with clever legal terminology may only serve to confuse most clients, and may backfire if the client feels that he is being talked down to or ends up so confused he decides not to proceed. Remember he is paying to obtain the firm's skills and knowledge and this is only a commodity which the firm is selling in competition with other firms. It is better to explain in a lay man's terms the ins and outs of the legal system, so as to manage the client's expectations.

2. Contacts

Next, the fee earner should let the client know who will be dealing with his file. If possible the client should meet the parties, albeit briefly to familiarise himself with them. The level of the person dealing the file should also be revealed, *i.e.* partner; fee earner of several years' experience; an expert in the particular field required; a junior or a trainee. There is nothing more galling for a client than finding that the partner who is an expert in the field for whom they came to the firm, is not the person dealing with the case, but that the work has actually been carried out by a trainee of little experience, (especially if he has been paying partner fee levels). Honesty in this situation goes a long way to helping build up a client relationship: *i.e.* that other members of staff will be working on the case and that the charges will be adjusted accordingly.

3 The Timetable

If there are statutory limitations to consider with regard to litigation cases, or deadlines in corporate matters, these should be discussed with the client and a timetable drawn up with the client so that both he and the solicitor concerned are working to the same time scale.

4 Responsibility

Documentation and information required from the client, should be discussed and it should be made clear to the client that they are responsible for providing the same and that their case can only be progressed with that information. The fee-earner should also explain to the client what documentation he will need to produce. In this way, the client and fee-earner achieve an agreed outline of responsibilities that create co-operation between them in progressing the case. This sense of co-operation can spill over to financial aspects of the case.

5 Financial aspects of the case

Fee levels

The initial meeting is the best opportunity to discuss the financial arrangement that a fee earner will make with the client. Clients going into this first meeting will be receptive to ideas and often will expect financial matters to be discussed. A fee earner should be as open as possible with the client about the potential cost of his case. Fee levels – how much per hour, how much for a letter etc – need to be discussed. If any uplifts are to be added for care and conduct, this needs to be brought to the client's attention and an explanation of what they are for and how the figures are arrived at needs to be made. Care and conduct uplifts when not known about by a client serve to irritate and can be the basis for the bill to be sent to taxation, which will of course only diminish the value of the work undertaken.

Funding

How the case is to be funded needs to be clearly understood. Will the client be eligible for legal aid? If so, will he have to make any contributions and will he be charged for pre-certificate work? It is not unknown for clients to leave the initial meeting without a clear understanding of where their legal aid starts and the private bills end. It is unfair to the client and financially unsound for the practice to fudge such areas. Clarity is essential. There is noone more difficult to extract funds from than a confused debtor. It takes the fee earner valuable fee earning time to try sort out the confusion, and the administration time of the credit controller in trying to chase the fee earner and the client to get the bill paid. Invariably it turns out that the client has not got the funds to pay anyway.

The potential for such confusion is enhanced by no win, no fee agreements in civil litigation. Well drafted agreements and legal protection insurance information may make things clear for some clients – but there will be an equal number who require terms explained to them. Indeed, one thing that fee earners have to be particularly wary of is how to communicate their own uncertainty as they make risk calculations on behalf of the firm, in a way that is fair to the client.[1]

The risks undertaken by the client

If the fee earner feels that the client is putting himself at a financial risk, he should point this out. It could be that the client is embarking on expensive litigation which if lost could be financially disastrous. On occasion even the costs of setting up the action could financially disable a client. In this situation, the fee earner has to make a value judgement as to whether he wants to take the risk of having a client who may not be able to finance his case – *i.e. pay the firm* – or whether it would be better not to take up the work at all.

Arrangements for billing

The first interview is the ideal opportunity to discuss and agree billing arrangements and the funding of expenses and disbursements. If possible interim bills should be arranged, though this will depend on the type of work undertaken. Such arrangements should be based on either a monetary value (for instance every time a ceiling of £500 or £1000 is reached) or a time value (for instance once a month or once a quarter). The agreements should be based on both the financial requirements of the practice and the financial resources of the client. It is sometimes easier for a client to find £1000 a month for ten months, than is it for him to find £10,000 in one month.

Disbursements

As clearly stated in the Solicitor's Accounts Rules 1991, legal practices are responsible for disbursements and expenses incurred during the course of a case and the fee earner should ensure that the client agrees to see that the practice is reimbursed for its expenditure as soon as possible, if not paid in

---

[1] For a clear and practical explanation of these matters, including advice on client interviewing and cash flow management, see *No Win, No Fee – No Worries* by Kerry Underwood, CLT Professional Publishing 1998

advance. The firm is responsible whether the client has made funds available to cover expenses or not. If fee-earners fail to take on board that the practice is responsible for the payment of disbursements they may find themselves in the following circumstances:

> Slap Dash & Co have a litigation case concerning work done by an engineering company. Their client is suing for remuneration for work undertaken but have encountered a counterclaim, alleging poor workmanship. Both counsel and engineering experts are instructed to help with the case. No agreement has been made with regard to the payment of disbursements as they occur. During the course of the case, the client goes into liquidation. Slap Dash & Co have therefore to find payment for counsel and the expert's fees out of their own pocket.

Credit terms or methods of payment should also be agreed with an explanation that they are non negotiable once the bill is issued under those terms.

Remember the balancing act: it is good to take into account the client cash flow – but don't forget the practice's own.

Estimates of cost
Quotations should be realistic. Legal services are increasingly competitive, but is foolhardy to give a cheap quote just to secure the work and then hope that during the course of the matter the client will agree to further charges. Sometimes they will not and will insist that the practice sticks to the quote given. If a quotation is given and there is a possibility that the case may suddenly take an alternative route which will incur further expense, then this should be made clear to the client. The practice should in its agreement maintain the right to reassess its charges, with a suitable opportunity for consideration by, and then authority from, the client. It is no good continuing with a case incurring further costs on the client's behalf, if the client is not prepared to fund the costs involved.

6   Complaints procedures

Clients need to know who to go to if they have a complaint. Being open about a complaints procedure does not necessarily make the client think that the fee earners are often the subject of complaint! Methods and time scales for dealing with queries should be clearly set out.

7   Database information

Once the details of the case are discussed and the client is comfortable, other information must be collected (if it has not arisen in the course of discussion). The most basic factors to be discussed will be the client's personal details such as name and address, work details. These items will be needed for the client database (details on setting up a database are given in Part 3).

8   Any other business

The end of the meeting should deal with any points arising from the discussion with the client. Any queries the client may have can be dealt with here. Also the fine tuning of the agreement can be gone over at this stage, so that both client and fee earner are in no doubt as to what has been agreed in relation to who is doing the work, at what rate, the framework and the financing of the case. A timetable for confirmation letters – or formal documented agreements such as quotations or conditional fee agreements – should also be agreed.

Has the Aim of the Meeting been Achieved?

What the initial meeting should have done is establish a rapport between client and fee earner. Both parties should know what is expected from the other and hopefully a long and mutually beneficial relationship can be commenced.

After the Meeting

After the meeting (obviously if the client has decided to proceed) all that has been agreed should be put in writing and either signed straight away by both parties or else sent to the client. Ideally work should not commence until the client has sent back his part of the agreement signed. The agreement, contract or client care letter (depending on what a practice chooses to call the document) should cover all the points discussed in the meeting. It can either be presented as a contract with a covering letter or be incorporated into a letter. However, the layout and style should be as clear as possible so that the client is left in no doubt as to what has been agreed.

An example agreement is set out overleaf. A precedent letter can be also be found on page 22 and on the optional disk: reference L1, with variations for firm quotations and no win, no fee agreements at L2 and L3.

A Firm & Co
Client Agreement

OUR AIMS
We aim to offer all our clients an efficient and effective service. This document is intended to explain the terms upon which we undertake business and the basis upon which our fees are calculated. We believe that this will avoid any possible misunderstandings later, and if any aspect is not clear, please contact the person dealing with your work.

PERSONNEL
Your case will be conducted by our Mr Jones. Mr Johnson will be the partner assigned with overall responsibility for the work undertaken on your behalf. As mentioned in our meeting there may be times when other colleagues will deal with aspects of your case, but they will have undergone the necessary training and will make themselves familiar with your file without charge to yourself. You will of course be informed of any changes that occur in personnel.

PROGRESS OF MATTERS
At the outset of each matter, we will discuss with you what is to be achieved and what is necessary to achieve it. Any material developments in the course of the matter, delays, or possible deviations from your instructions will always be reported to you, but we will be guided by you as to the extent to which you wish us to report in detail otherwise.

FEES
With regard to our fees you will remember that they are based on the amount of time spent by the personnel engaged on your matter. Each member of our staff has an hourly rate which forms the basis of our fees, and these rates are reviewed annually. However, because each individual matter presents its own unique characteristics, our fee may be adjusted upwards or downwards to take account of factors such as the complexity, importance or value of the matter, its urgency or novelty. We will of course refer to you and be guided by your instructions. We aim to charge a fair fee in all the circumstances. Where a client has agreed a particular basis of charging with us, this will, of course, be adhered to. If for any reason we cease to act before a matter has been completed, we shall be entitled to charge for all work done up to that point.

Please let us know immediately if you consider that your legal fees may be covered by insurance or Legal Aid, or if there are any changes in your circumstances which could affect this.

PAYMENT OF COSTS

So far as disbursements are concerned, such as search fees, counsel's or expert's fees, court fees etc, we would like to receive these prior to being paid out by the firm and we will notify you before they are incurred.

Clients will be billed at the completion of the matter, unless the amount of costs outstanding reaches £500, in which case an interim bill will be submitted which will be marked as such. An interim bill may also be submitted at some other appropriate stage by prior agreement with you. Value Added Tax will be added to all accounts.

We agreed that you would make payments on account of anticipated costs and, it is helpful if you can meet requests promptly, but if there is any difficulty please let us know as soon as possible.

Settlement of our bills is due within 30 days of presentation and we reserve the right to charge interest at an annual rate of 8% above base lending rate on bills not paid[1] within that time. We also reserve the right to discontinue work on all your current matters if any bill is not settled promptly.

On matters where a third party has agreed to pay your legal costs, these still remain your responsibility should the third party fail for any reason to settle the account.

ORDER FOR COSTS

In matters involving litigation, if the action is successful it may be that you will be entitled to the payment of your costs by some other party. However, it is rare for the system of "taxation" of costs to result in the losing party having to pay the full amount of your costs. As a general guide, you may expect to recover two-thirds of your costs by these means, but this is a complex subject and we would be happy to explain it further if you wish.

QUESTIONS AND COMPLAINTS

We hope that you will be completely satisfied with the service we offer, but if you have any questions or complaints about our work or our charges, or if you are troubled by any aspect of the matter, please feel free to contact the partner with responsibility for your work or our Senior Partner Mr Firm.

---

1 The Late Payment of Commercial Debts (Interest) Act 1998 – see further page 23.

A Firm & Co
BarcWest Chambers
High Street
Northbridge

Mrs Client
34 Harrobim Road
Northbridge

Dear Mrs Client

<u>Housing Action Against Northbridge Borough Council</u>

I thank you for your instructions and confirm that we will be pleased to act on your behalf in relation to seeking repairs to your housing and damages (if available) for the delays in such repairs, with the consequent effects on your health. My colleagues and I will make every effort to ensure that matters proceed as smoothly as possible. I enclose a copy of our Terms of Business, which the Law Society require us to provide to all clients and should be grateful if you would please confirm that these are acceptable, by signing and returning to me a copy of this letter in the enclosed prepaid envelope.

I shall carry out most of the work personally, but you can also contact John Johnson, a Partner with the firm, and who will be familiar with ongoing files. If he is unable to help you he will be pleased to take a message for you. Alternatively, you are welcome to contact my secretary, Jenny Green, who will endeavour to assist you.

Yours sincerely

Gwyn Jones
Solicitor

I have read, understood and agree to A. Firm & Co's terms of business as set out in their Client Agreement.

Signed .... Date ....

Print Name ....

Late Payment of Commercial Debts (Interest) Act 1998

Smaller practices who have not included a provision for interest against late payers in their contracts can now look to a new Act passed by the government in November 1998. The Late Payment of Commercial Debts (Interest) Act 1998 gives small businesses regardless of legal status a statutory right to claim interest against large businesses and public sectors on debts incurred under contracts agreed after 1st November 1998. The Act has been developed to protect smaller enterprises against the powerful larger companies who have in the past been able to stretch their smaller suppliers by extending credit terms to suit themselves. This extension of credit is perceived to be one of the causes of the failure of many small businesses.

A small business is defined in the Act as one with under 50 full time employees. If no credit terms in the contract have been agreed the Act sets a default at 30 days from the later of two actions: the performance of the service; or the date on which the invoice is issued.

The rate of interest the Act allows to be charged is Bank of England base rate + 8% on the final day of the credit term.

Note that claims for interest do not have to be made straight away: the Act gives the supplier of the service six years in England to register a claim. (Five years for Scotland.) Interest can be claimed from the client regardless of whether a practice has ceased to act for them.

As with any overdue invoice the practice has the right to take the client to court for non payment of the interest element. Of course the practice must ensure that the client was correctly notified of all charges and that no queries have been left outstanding.

What if the Client Gives Further Instructions?

Each time a client gives new instructions to the practice, a letter should be sent confirming the instructions and referring the client back to the original agreement he signed. The client should be allowed the opportunity to go over the terms and conditions of the relationship again. A sample of such a letter is set out overleaf and on disk, at L4.

A Firm & Co
BarcWest Chambers
High Street
Northbridge

Mrs Client
34 Harrobim Road
Northbridge

Dear Mrs Client

<u>Action against Northbridgshire County Council to reverse C. Client's exclusion from school</u>

I thank you for your instructions and confirm that we will be pleased to act on your behalf in relation to your son's exclusion from Northbridge High School. My colleagues and I will make every effort to ensure that matters proceed as smoothly as possible. You will already have received a copy of our Terms of Business, which the Law Society require us to provide to all clients, but please advise should you wish to receive a further copy.

I shall carry out most of the work personally, but you can also contact John Johnson, a Partner in the firm, and who will be familiar with ongoing files. If he is unable to help you he will be pleased to take a message for you. Alternatively, you are welcome to contact my secretary, Jenny Green, who will endeavour to assist you.

I would be grateful if you would confirm you accept these terms and conditions, by signing and returning to me a copy of this letter in the enclosed prepaid envelope.

Yours sincerely

Gwyn Jones
Solicitor

I have read, understood and agree to A. Firm & Co's terms of business as set out in their Client Agreement.

Signed ....

Print Name ....

Summary

Establishing the ground rules for a future relationship must be done at the first meeting. It is very difficult once the work is underway to try and obtain payments on account of disbursement or send interim bills when no arrangement of this nature has been made with the client in advance. The client relationship *must* be set up in a professional manner.

Achievements

It should now be appreciated:

1. Why it is important to establish the ground rules in the client relationship
2. How to set an agenda to cover the ground rules at the first and an annual client meeting
3. How to provide a written confirmation of what has been agreed in a form understandable to the client.

Chapter 2

Minimising Financial Exposure

Introductory	28
Objectives	28
The importance of risk assessment	29
Summary	30
Achievements	31

Chapter 2

Minimising Financial Exposure

Introductory

Establishing a clear understanding of the undertakings of client and fee earner is the first step in controlling, monitoring and maximising profitability through improved cash flow. The next step is to ensure the protection of the financial exposure of the practice to bad debt. A legal practice usually offers an unsecured credit period for its bills, and often incurs disbursements on behalf of the client. Sometimes this is done without either checking who the client is or obtaining monies on account. Most businesses today do not allow complete strangers to walk into their premises and buy items without paying in advance, or having some assurance that their credit will be good. There is no reason why a legal practice should be any different. It is pointless working on files, building up disbursements and costs, if the client is not going to be able to meet his obligations when the bill is presented to him. The Practice is the one under obligation to pay the disbursements incurred not the client. Put bluntly, the client who will not pay, will not be troubled if the practice is put into financial difficulties because of persistent bad debts.

> **Objectives**
>
> On completing this chapter, the reader should:
>
> 1 Understand why the practice needs to be protected from unnecessary financial exposure
> 2 Be aware of the methods for so doing

The importance of risk assessment

It is essential that a risk assessment is carried out by the fee earner before embarking on work on behalf of the client. Every bad debt costs the practice profit. This occurs through loss of working capital, reducing the available funds for re-investment (and draw down). Eventually this could lead to down sizing, a smaller share in the market sector and in the most extreme case closure of the practice.

In order to protect the practice from unnecessary exposure the fee earner should bear the following points in mind:

1. As much as possible should be known about the client
2. The fee earner (or the accounts) department should set credit limits and stick to them
3. The fee earner should ensure that the financial arrangements made at the initial meeting are adhered to.

1 Who is the client?

It is a sensible precaution to know to whom the practice is offering its services, and to establish whether the client will be able to meet their obligations. This can be done using a number of methods, which range in cost from nothing to a few pounds. The most obvious method relates to the case. If the matter relates to an Individual Voluntary Arrangement or bankruptcy or an employment problem, then the fee earner should seriously consider obtaining money on account!

Another factor which the fee earner should take into consideration is if the business client's case will cause him/his company financial hardship. If the fee earner considers that it will then again, monies should be obtained as the case progresses.

Other methods of client risk assessment will include references, usually banking ones, or credit checks (these are discussed on page 79). Fee earners should be able to balance client care with practice care when embarking on risk assessment. The aim should be to protect the practice, not lose the client.

2   Sticking to the credit limits

A sensible and workable credit limit should be set on each client, and adhered to by the fee earner. It is not unknown for fee earners to continue working on cases long after the credit limit has been passed only to find that the client has gone into liquidation. It is better that when a credit limit is reached the client is billed (it could be that the client has agreed to interim billing in any case) and that no further expense is incurred until that bill is cleared. This way the exposure risk remains at a minimum.

Credit limits like, the client relationship, should be reviewed at least once a year to take into consideration:

- the client's current status
- their payment record to date and
- their overall value to the practice in terms of their own work and the introduction of further clients to the practice.

All these items should be taken into consideration. If a client has had a good payment history and is deemed to be financially sound, an increase in the level of credit may be made.

3   Financial arrangements should be stuck to

If the client breaks any of the financial arrangements agreed at the initial meeting the fee earner should stop work. The arrangement was put in place for the protection and benefit of both client and practice.

Summary

Each fee earner has a duty to protect his practice from unnecessary bad debt. Risk assessment is neither expensive nor difficult and should be undertaken for all clients.

Achievements

The reader should now:

1 Understand why the practice needs to be protected from unnecessary financial exposure
2 Appreciate the methods for so doing

Chapter 3

Maximising the Value of the File

Objectives	34
What does the firm sell?	34
Time	34
Disbursements	35
Working within the Parameters of the Initial Agreement	35
General File Discipline	36
Achievements	36

Chapter 3

Maximising the Value of the File

Once the fee earner has agreed the terms of the relationship with the client and undertaken risk assessment, the next step is to ensure that *maximum value* for the work is obtained.

> ### Objectives
>
> Having completed this chapter, individuals should:
>
> 1. Understand why it is important to have maximum value for work undertaken
> 2. Appreciate the methods by which this can be achieved

What does the firm sell?

As a factory has wood for making furniture to sell, a legal practice has client files from which comes saleable value. Client files are the life blood of the legal practice and as such their value as a source of revenue should be understood. Given that there are only so many working hours in a day, as high a proportion as possible of these should be chargeable.

Time

Most fee earners sell their skill in units of time, so it is sensible that they should charge (obviously within the parameters of the client agreement) for all the time spent working on a file. The most common method of accounting time is time sheets, whether using automated time keeping or a paper-based system. Whatever method used, it is essential that the information entered is accurate and put onto the right file. Fee earners must take responsibility to put the correct name and file number and work type onto the time sheets. If time is entered onto the wrong file, it can miss a billing run.

In addition, clients may ask for copies of time transactions to support the fees billed. It is therefore most sensible to fill out time sheets (or put the time on the system) as it is done. If left for days it is easy to miss off units of times; it is not unknown for whole days of time to go missing. Time which is not accounted may never be recovered; the practice has then lost profits.

Disbursements

All disbursement/expenses incurred on behalf of the client should be accounted for to the client and entered onto the file. What should never be allowed to happen is that practice pays out for a disbursement and is not able to recover it from the client. Care should always be taken to keep copies of disbursement invoices on file, with notes of payments. In this way if proof of expenses is asked for the client, it is readily available.

Working within the Parameters of the Initial Agreement

Professionals know that the instruction comes from the client and the solicitor is acting in the client's interests. In financial terms this means that the client has his hand on the purse strings. No matter how interesting the case, or whether the fee earner thinks that if the client is willing to spend a little more he will win, the client has to be allowed the choice of where he wants his case to go. If, for example, the case takes an unexpected turn and is going to cost more than the quote, the client should be told straight away. This way he can make the choice as to whether he will continue to fund it or not. The fee earner must not make that decision for him, and then present the client with a fait accompli bill. It will spoil the relationship and the bill will probably end up being credited back to the original quotation level or written off. The fee earner has to work within the parameters agreed.

General File Discipline

It is usual for most fee earners to separate their files into two halves: correspondence and notes, and financial matters. This system will help the fee earner monitor the expenses incurred. It is essential that a fee earner keeps up to date with all financial transactions be they counsel's fees or the transfer of client funds. It is much easier to keep account on a day to day basis than to have to sort through mounds of documentation, (wasting valuable fee earning time) when it comes to billing the client.

Files which are correctly managed and maintained will present the fee earner with no problems when embarking on a billing run, and should yield maximum value.

Achievements

The practice needs fee-earners to:

1 Understand the importance of regular time-recording
2 Understand the value of regular, disciplined review of financial transactions on a file
3 Ensure disbursements and expenses are charged efficiently and back-up retained
4 Work within the parameters of the client agreement, reporting and obtaining agreement for any variances
5 Understand the methods of achieving these objectives.

Chapter 4

The Billing Stage

Objectives	38
What is a Bill?	38
When is it Appropriate to Raise a Bill?	39
Billing and Disbursements	40
Two Types of Bill	40
The Formatting of the Bill	42
The Finishing Touch	47
Achievements	47

Chapter 4

The Billing Stage

One of the most common complaints with regard to a Legal Practice's bills is that the bills themselves are unclear, and the charges unsupported. This chapter is intended to be a guide to better billing. It covers the explanation of what a bill is and when it is appropriate to raise one. Also covered are the issues which should be addressed prior to the bill being raised.

> ## Objectives
>
> At the end of this section you should appreciate:
>
> 1. What a bill is
> 2. When it is appropriate to raise the bill
> 3. Which types of bill should be raised and when
> 4. Which financial transactions will need to take place prior to the bill being sent out
> 5. The format of the bill and backing schedules

What is a Bill?

A bill is a statement of charges for goods or services. It is a document which must clearly let the client know:

- how much they owe
- for what they are paying
- to whom it is payable; and
- when to pay it.

It is an inherent part of the file, not an afterthought. The bill should be every bit as professional in appearance and content as the work carried out on the file for the client. In some cases the bill is the last point of contact between the fee earner and the client. Careless and inaccurate billing can lead the client to doubt the quality of the services he has received, which will compromise the chances of new instructions. Such doubt can also lead to slow payment, taxation or non-payment.

If the above factors are taken into consideration, then the fee earner will be able to provide to his client a clear, accurate and concise financial statement. The client should then be unable to delay payment with pleas of confusion or requests for breakdowns.

*The fee earner should remember that a file has only been truly completed when the bill is **remunerated**.*

When is it Appropriate to Raise a Bill?

The timing of bills must take a number of factors into account:

- The current position of the matter
- The level of credit extended with WIP
- Disbursements
- Any unpaid bill previously rendered; and
- The agreement with the client.

Note: A fee earner's billing targets should not be the overriding factor when deciding to raise a bill. A bill that is raised purely on the basis of the need to achieve targets without due regard to the client agreement is likely to be of less use to the practice in making profits. If anything a bill raised in this manner will cost the practice profit, both in terms of the worsening of the client relationship and administration charges. It is not uncommon for 'target bills' to end up being credited, usually several months later and after several (expensive) letters to and/ or discussions with the client.

Bills should only be raised if they are going to be paid within the specified credit terms of the practice. If the file has reached a point where it can and should be billed (*i.e.* reached the credit limit or the quotation or the matter is complete), and if the client is expecting and has agreed to be billed, there should be no problem obtaining payment within those specified terms.

A bill should be raised as soon as the matter is completed – within 48 hours – whilst it is still fresh in both the fee-earner's and client's minds and the relationship is current. Bills raised at a later date give the client a longer period of credit and allow them to forget what a good job the fee earner did for them.

A further note on cash flow and billing

The fee earner should remember that if raising a bill with payment contingent on a sale of an asset, VAT is payable from the tax point (date) on the bill: not when the bill is paid. This should particularly be noted by fee earners dealing with domestic conveyances who bill prior to completion.

Billing and Disbursements

All disbursements that arise in the course of a matter should be billed to the client irrespective of whether there has been a payment in advance. The client will need an accurate account of payments made for his own records. If payment has been made in advance this should be clearly stated in words on the bill, the figures should have either a minus sign, or be denoted in brackets to show payment has been received, thus balancing the bill to zero, or clearly showing the outstanding balance.

Two Types of Bill

There are two types of bill which a fee earner can raise. These are:

- An interim bill; and
- A final bill.

Raising the correct bill at the right time is an essential element of obtaining maximum value for work carried out by the fee earner. Sending the client a 'final' bill when he should have had an 'interim' bill can cause not only confusion to the client but can also lead to difficulties in obtaining payment when the fee earner sends another 'final' bill at the end of the case.

Interim Bills

These will be most commonly used by corporate and litigation departments where matters tend to be protracted, and wherever the client has specified a ceiling on costs. The frequency of these interim bills will depend on either triggers based on monetary value or based on a time period: this should have been discussed at the initial client meeting. As this type of billing protects the practice from prolonged exposure to the risk of the client defaulting and also protects the client's own cash flow, the fee earner should undertake to send out these bills at the appropriate times. He should not be tempted to leave them for one more month or decide to bill at the end of the file, because it shows both a lack of regard for the client's cash flow *and* puts the practice in a financially exposed position. Furthermore the fee earner will be contravening the client agreement.

The fee earner should take note of whether payment is made within the terms of the agreement or if it is delayed. It is financially advisable that, if payment is not forthcoming, the fee earner should not continue with the case until the client does make payment. It is sometimes the case that if the client does not keep his pre-arranged interim billing arrangements, it is an indicator of financial difficulties. If the fee earner continues to work, the practice will be exposed to further levels of unprotected credit which may not be recoverable.

Final Bills

Final bills should only be raised when the matter has been completed. They should clearly be marked 'final bill'. This is the last chance for a fee earner will have to charge the client for all time, disbursements and expenses incurred during the conduct of his case: nothing should be missed.

Pre-Billing Financial Checklist

- All time sheets should be accounted for
- All disbursements incurred on the file should be noted, with particular attention being made as to whether they have been paid by the client prior to bill issue
- Any client to office transactions which need to be carried out should be and be included and noted on the final calculations
- The bill issued should reflect the true financial statement of the file.

It is up to the fee earner to check his accounts system against his file prior to the issuing of the bill out to the client. Nothing should be left off it. It is very difficult to go back to a client, once the final bill has been issued, to ask for further funds on account of lost time sheets!

The Formatting of the Bill

Any bill presented to a client should be of a high standard, both in presentation and content. There are a number of different formats used by solicitors. Some use two columns, showing Fees and Disbursements in the same column, with the second being used for VAT. Others use three columns which split the costs and disbursements clearly into separate columns with third column being used for the VAT elements of both. What a bill will look like in terms of design is up to the practice – as long as the information contained in it is clear and disbursements are shown separately from the fees elements.

If in doubt the practice should ask a range of clients what they find clear and unclear about the way they are billed.

What Should Be Included

A bill is an important financial document. It should not be cluttered with unnecessary detail.

Below is a checklist of the *only* details which should appear on it:

1. Client's name and address
2. Date
3. Practice reference, *i.e.* matter number & fee earner's initials.
4. Client's own reference
5. Financial calculations
   Clearly showing the amount to be paid less any amounts that have been paid in advance.
6. Brief narrative:
   Stating which matter the bill relates to, and clearly identifying all cost details, *i.e.* all disbursements such as counsel's fees
7. Payment terms
8. Whether VAT is applicable.

Forms of address

The name and address of the client for whom the work has been undertaken should be entered onto the bill. The fee earner should have ensured that his client information is accurate and up to date with regard to addresses and name changes during the course of his file, but particular attention should be paid to these matters at billing time to ensure that there is no delay in payment.

For the sake of good client relations matters of a sensitive nature, *e.g.* employment disputes, company takeovers etc, should be clearly identified as 'Private & Confidential' and the name of the contact should be clearly marked on the bill. This will avoid any unauthorised person gaining sight of the document. A further way of protecting confidential matters would be to use only the client's reference on the face of the bill, with a generalised heading such as "General Employment Matter" in an employment case. With regard to other matters, it maybe that even private clients will sometimes pass accounts to a third party to pay and so it is better that long description of the cases are not put onto the bill face. As the bill is purely a financial document case description should not be featured on it.

If a bill is payable by a third party this should be noted on the bill – in order that the right party be chased for payment.

References

It is the purpose of the bill to "help" clients pay the practice. The client's own reference must be clearly shown on the face of the bill. This is particularly the case if the client is either a Corporate Body or an Insurance Company. It should alway be understood that the practice will not be the only creditor of the client and in some cases there may be several claims going on at the same time, each one being handled by a different person. Confusion will delay payment and may cause embarrassment.

Financial information

The following steps must be carried out prior to billing:

- Time and disbursements must be checked for accuracy before the billing process begins
- Client to office transfers should be initiated when rendering the bill if the client has previously approved the bill
- All calculations should be carefully checked
- Monies received on account should be shown on the bill as having been allocated to the final total using brackets round the figures and clearly indicating "'less on account of [whatever has been paid, *e.g.* Writ Fee]"
- VAT must be calculated correctly and checked

Inaccurate financial information has two effects. Firstly it make the fee earner look sloppy. Secondly, it gives the client a opportunity to delay payment. If the fee earner wishes his bills to return maximum profitability to the practice he should ensure that only information that is 100% accurate should be used in the billing process.

Breakdowns and completion statements
Whereas the bill will let the client know how much he owes and to whom he should pay it, the fee earner should also provide the client with a breakdown of how he reached his figures. A detailed schedule should accompany all bills issued to the client, even if the amount rendered is in line with an earlier quotation. There should be two breakdowns, one for costs and one for disbursements and an example of each is shown. These are also set out on disk at P1 and P2 on the following pages. Whilst it is up to the individual practice how the schedules are styled, they should follow the format of being clear and easily understandable to the client. The schedules should be headed by the name and matter number of the client, with the description of the matter unless it is of a confidential nature.

If in any doubt as to the worth of schedules the fee earner should bear in mind that breakdowns serve a twofold purpose:

1. to substantiate the fee rendered
2. to stop the client from requesting a breakdown which is a common method of delaying payment

Schedule of Costs

Client Name: Matter No:

Re:

14.5.97	Letter from [name]	10 minutes
18.5.97	Letter to [client name]	20 minutes
21.5.97	Telephone call to [Name]	10 minutes
25.5.97	Drafting Court Order	60 minutes
26.5.97	Telephone call [Name]	5 minutes
1.6.97	Court attendance & waiting time	180 minutes
4.6.97	Letter to [Name]	5 minutes
5.6.97	Letter to [Name]	10 minutes

Total Time 5 hours @ £110 per hour = £550 plus VAT

Schedule of Disbursements

Client Name: Matter No:
Re:

VATable:	£
Counsel's Fees	450.00
VAT	78.75
Non VATable:	
Company Search Fee	6.60
Total Disbursements	£535.35

The Finishing Touch

Before either a final or interim bill is sent out, a telephone call should be made to the client, advising of the level of charges levied, referring to any quotation previously given. Any queries or misunderstanding as to what the quotation was, or the service given, can be ironed out at this stage, rather than after the arrival of the bill. Money is an emotive subject, and it is helpful to the payment process if the fee earner can spend a few minutes on the telephone preparing the client for the bill. This gives the opportunity for the client to agree the charges and the fee earner to be able to issue his bill in the knowledge that it will be paid within the practice's credit terms.

> *Achievements*
>
> The practice needs its fee earners and relevant staff to understand:
>
> 1   What a bill is
> 2   When it is appropriate to raise the bill
> 3   Which types of bill to raise and when
> 4   The financial transactions which will need to take place prior to the bill being sent out
> 5   How to format the bill and backing schedules

Part II

The Credit Management System

Part II

The Credit Management System

Why Set Up A Credit Management System?	52
The Aim of the Policy	52
Your Place in The Credit Queue	53
Team Work	54
Everybody Should Understand The Importance Of Debtors	54

Part II

The Credit Management System

If You Don't Ask... You Won't Get

Why Set Up A Credit Management System?

You could be forgiven for thinking that by following all the pre billing steps you can just sit back and watch the fees roll in. Unfortunately, life isn't that simple! It is generally accepted that in the UK payment is as slow as anywhere in Europe. Invoices are regularly paid late by days, weeks or even months after their specified credit terms, regardless of whether the bill was agreed. Allowing this to happen can have a serious impact on the practice. So, for example, if the bill is paid 35 days late, the practice would be penalised 35 days' worth of interest in relation to bank overdraft charges or lost interest on credit balances. Following the guidelines in the first section will help in as much as they will 'oil' the cogs of the payment process, (*i.e.* stop stalling tactics – like asking for breakdowns or haggling for discounts, which may weeks to sort out) but unless the firm has an exceptional client base it will find that the clients will try to delay payment for long as possible and certainly the client will try turn your credit terms into their credit terms.

The Aim of the Policy

As with anything in business the secret of success is in the planning. You have to be able to identify where you are and where you want to be. Examine the resources available to the firm then draw up and implement the necessary steps. It is not possible to run a successful collections system if there is not a policy or any specified procedures. It would be a bit like jumping out of a plane without a parachute: exceptionally dangerous and ultimately disastrous.

The first goal of any decent Credit Management System is to produce an effective and efficient collections strategy, which whilst producing optimum cash flow, will not compromise or harm client relations. However, the good and well thought out Credit Management System will not just be a directive on how to go about collecting money, but should also encompass:

- customer care
- personnel and training
- financial and trend analysis
- exposure detection
- WIP and disbursement management
- cash flow projections, and, perhaps surprisingly
- marketing information for cross selling purposes.

Long gone are the days when the credit control was just about collecting debts!

Your Place In The Credit Queue

Collecting credit is a competitive business and it is necessary to understand that your firm is not usually the client's only creditor. In terms of corporate clients there will be a long queue of creditors both in front and behind your firm. Finance Directors and the like always will put a solicitor's bill behind a supplier of necessary raw materials. No matter how good a job was done on the lease, management buy out or litigation action, the services which have been provided therefore cannot be turned into a tangible profit making item. The firm may have saved the client's company, but it can still go to the back of the queue for payment! Even private clients will have other bills beside their solicitors, which they may feel are more pressing. If you want your firm to be paid within the terms agreed or as soon after that as possible, you are going to have to be prepared to *ask* for it systematically.

Part II is intended as a guide to help you create and develop an efficient, effective and professional collection system using the accounts packages and personnel resources available to you. Once a credit system is set up your firm will find that not only will it speed up payment processes but it will identify debtor problems sooner rather than later.

Team Work

It should be noted that a successful Credit Management System is dependent on team work between the collector and the fee earner. The debtors ledger is not a battle ground to be fought over, it is not about power struggles or office politics, but about gaining maximum profitably for the practice. Clients will, if allowed, set off a chain of interdepartmental wrangles over who said what and whether extended payment terms were offered: "Mr Jones who handled my case said I didn't have to pay until I get paid my rent/ tax rebate/ debtors funds etc etc ".

All this does is breed bad feeling between the fee earner – trying to protect his/her client – and the credit controller wanting to collect the practice's money. The only winner of this situation is the client who is able to get away with non payment for however long it takes to sort out the internal bickering. Doubtless if that same client supplies your practice with goods, rest assured that he will want paying within his terms and he won't be allow non payment with excuses like 'We're waiting for a case to complete!'.

Everybody Should Understand The Importance Of Debtors

Remember the debtors ledger is one of the most important assets a legal firm has and should be treated as such by both fee earner and credit controller alike. It is not acceptable for anybody to offer longer credit terms or special favours for their particular clients. If one does it, it may not matter. If everybody does it the firm can say goodbye to its cash flow.

It is essential that you have a written policy that is presented to everybody and adhered to by everybody with no exceptions.

There will alway be late payers: just how late they are going to be is entirely up to you. The sooner you devise and implement a credit system, the sooner you can begin to dictate to your clients when they will pay you, instead if vice versa.

Once you have read the following chapters you should be able to:

1. Understand why it is important to have a credit policy and collections system
2. Create a suitable policy and collections system for your practice
3. Implement the practical collection procedures most suitable for you using the resources available to you
4. Train staff (both accounts and fee earners) in the art of credit collection

Chapter 5

Creating The Policy

The Credit Management Policy 58
Present The Document To All Staff 63

Chapter 5

Creating The Policy

The creation of an effective Credit Management System should be split into two separate but co-existing areas: *policy* and *procedures*. Procedures are dealt with in Chapter 6.

The Credit Management Policy

Obviously the content of the Credit Management Policy will depend on the individual circumstances of the practice, but any policy should state the following in clear and certain terms:

1. Who is to collect the debts
2. What is the reporting structure
3. How much working capital the firm is prepared to have tied up in debtors
4. Whether interest is to be charged on the late payment of debts and at what rate
5. What the firm's credit terms are
6. How the firm is going to control exposure levels for the clients
7. What the policy is regarding disbursements and the payment thereof

1 Who is going to chase the debts

This will depend very much on the resources available to the practice. It maybe that the turnover and client base is sufficiently large to warrant a team of credit controllers, or that the work can be done by one credit controller. It maybe that it will be sufficient for a member of staff such as a cashier, secretary or trainee, to control the debtor levels.

An educated guess at desirable staffing levels would be to have one collector for every 300 live accounts (or turnover of £3m) for a practice with a mixed Private Client and Corporate base. This is to encompass chasing by both telephone and letter cycle, both of which will be dealt with later on in Part II. The larger the turnover, the larger the number of live accounts to chase, and obviously then the number of credit controllers will have to increase to keep up with the work. An automatic credit control system will help reduce the number of personnel, but remember someone has to operate the system: it doesn't run and maintain its own records.

2 What is the reporting structure

Once it has been decided who is to chase the debts it must be made clear to whom they are to report. In most cases it would be appropriate for a particular partner (preferably one who is financially aware) to be appointed in charge of debtors. Obviously, if the practice has a full time accountant (or Financial Director) then they should be also be reported to directly by the Credit Controller. It is advisable that only one person makes the final decisions relating to debtors. If responsibility for debtors is split in several directions with different people making diverse and non-compatible decisions, all sorts of financial and client relations problems can ensue. If only one person has control this will be of benefit to the practice as they will know the overall position of the debtors and can make rational decisions based on whole picture.

A typical reporting structure for the smaller practice could be:

For the larger firm the reporting structure could look like this:

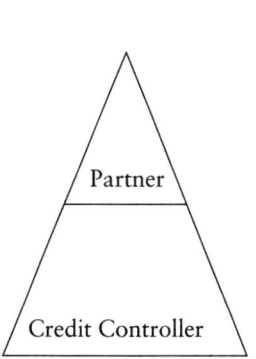
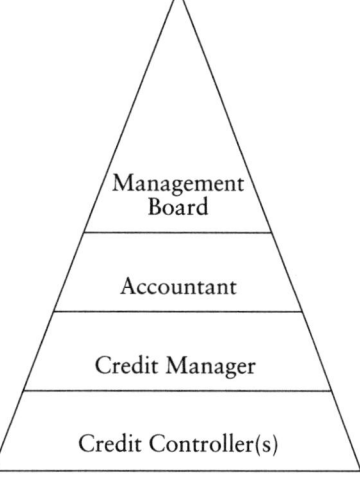

3 How much working capital are you prepared to have tied up debtors?

This section of the policy should state how much the firm is prepared to have invested in your debtors ledger at any one time. Again this depends entirely on the individual practice, but it can be expressed either:

- as a financial figure, *i.e.* £x out of an expected turnover of £x, or
- as debtor days, *i.e.* no more than 65 days fees outstanding.

4 Is interest to be charged on the late payment of debts?

The Late Payment of Commercial Debts (Interest) Act 1998 may apply to your practice if your client is a large or governmental organisation. For more on this Act see page 23.

A clear statement should be made on whether the firm is going to charge interest on late payers and if so:

- how this is going to be applied and
- how much is going to be charged.

The rate should be sufficiently high to act as a deterrent, but not so high as to make it unfair in the eyes of the court. Obviously the practice must make it clear to clients that it reserves the right to charge interest on late payments. The biggest difficulty with charging interest will be calculations and how to bill. Often it is considered that charging an interest penalty is more trouble than it is worth in relation to the time and effort to work it out and then bill it, but reserving the right to do so may help you with persistently bad payers. Sometimes the threat of interest charges persuades the client to part more quickly with their money.

5 Decide what the firm's credit terms are going to be

It is of vital importance that the firm decides what its credit terms are going to be and sticks to them. Once decided upon they should *not* be varied. There is very little point in getting clients used to 30 days and then deciding that the firm is going to change payment terms to 25 days. If the firm cannot make up its mind about its credit terms why should the client worry about sticking to them?

To decide what is a suitable credit term for your practice, take into account the local norm, *i.e.* how many days credit your nearest competitors offer. It may be that you would want to match theirs or again you may want to use your credit facility as a marketing incentive and offer longer periods of free credit. Remember though if you get into the credit facility "offers game", you could end up with all your competitors increasing their terms and you all end up getting paid later rather than sooner. Use your commercial sense. On the whole, 30 days is deemed to be a suitable period of credit in line with many other business outside of the legal world. There may be occasions where you forced to offer particular clients a longer term of credit, usually because in their own world their credit terms are longer and you wouldn't get the work otherwise: these should be the exception.

6 Decide how exposure levels will be controlled

Exposure levels for clients need to be implemented to protect the practice. This is a method of risk assessment, *i.e.* protection of the practice against unnecessary financial damage. Desirable levels of Work in Progress (WIP), Disbursements and outstanding accounts should be decided as soon as client has been taken on. It must be made clear who is to set the exposure level, or credit limit. Usually this will be the credit manager or accountant: for smaller practices it can be the partner in charge of debtors. The budget should then be set up at client level, *i.e.* not sub matter level (for reasons see page 77).

7 How are you going to fund Disbursements?

The firm's policy should state how it will finance disbursements. Will you ask the client for them in advance, or will you fund them and then ask your client for them at a later date? Again this is entirely up to the individual practice to decide but the former course is more advisable and kinder to your cash flow. If you do intend to make the client pay for disbursements rather than you funding them, then this must be conveyed to the client.

Once you have your policy strategy worked out, it must be written down and then adhered to by all the Fee Earners and made clear to the clients. There cannot be *any* exceptions or special favours for particular clients and for good reason. Take the following scenario for example:

> Slap Dash & Co have a Credit Management Policy which states that disbursements must be obtained from the client in advance.
>
> Quality Company Ltd has been using Slap Dash & Co for some time and has several on-going cases with two Fee Earners. One case requires £20,000 of Counsel's fees to be paid before Counsel will go into the hearing. The Fee Earner dealing with the case having read the Credit Management Policy relating to the funding of disbursements duly asks the client for the funds. The client is quite put out: the other Fee Earner never asks for funds in advance they are usually paid out the necessary funds and wait for reimbursement once the matter has completed, "and if Slap Dash & Co want to retain our business that's the way it's going to stay."
>
> The result of this is the client is unhappy, the Fee Earner is unhappy, and the practice will probably end up funding Quality Company's Counsel's bill until the end of the case, which could be several months down the line.

All of the above need careful consideration and deliberation and should be agreed upon, by the Partners, Accountant and Credit Manager (if you have one).

The Three P's – Proactive, Positive And Professional

Credit Management has a negative reputation in the eyes of more than a just a few fee earners. Many a fee earner has referred to their collections people rather less than politely as 'Rottweilers' or ask that 'the dogs be called off'. Interdepartmental conflict has no place in the modern practice and should be clearly addressed in the firm's Credit Management Policy.

Credit Management is about the three P's: staff that collect credit should all be as

- *Proactive,*
- *Positive* and
- *Professional*

as any fee earner. It should be made clear that the new policy to be implemented is not a method of subversively removing fee earner control over the client and replacing it with accounts people. Instead it should emphasise that accounts and the fee earner are working together in the pursuit of a single goal: *to get the bill paid.*

Present The Document To All Staff

Once the policy and procedures have been decided upon they should be presented to *all* the members of staff it affects, *i.e.* accounts, fee earners and secretarial staff. The latter members of the team are often left out of such training, which is short sighted as more often than not it is they who get to know first what is going on with the client, will have access to the files and notes that the credit collector may need to know prior to chasing. At these presentations any fears of 'power shifts' or 'toe-stepping' can be brought out in the open and alleviated. A Credit Management System should be openly practised and not be a secret agenda.

To assist in the presentation of the need for a Credit Management Policy and the structure and terms of the policy, presentation materials are available to complement this book.

Procedures

A detailed programme of the collections cycle and
how it is to be operated   66
How clients are to be financially assessed with
regard to risk management aka exposure levels   66

Procedures

The second stage of the Credit Management System should detail how the procedures are to be implemented. This should include the following:

1 **A detailed programme of the collections cycle and how it is to be operated**
   This section covers the setting up of the procedures system, the timing of the chasing cycle, the preferred chasing techniques to be used, and the various stages of communications that should be made between account chaser and fee earner along the way.

2 **How clients are to be financially assessed with regard to risk management**
   A detailed explanation of how the clients are to be financially assessed. That is, what type of credit checks is the firm going to carry out and who is to set the credit limit?
   The next two chapters are intended as guides to help practices – regardless of size – to produce a suitable set of procedures to implement their credit policy.
   It should be noted that once the procedures have been selected they should, like the policy itself, be adhered to by all. There is little point in having a set of rules if there is going to be several members of staff doing their own thing.

Chapter 6

Selecting Suitable Chasing Procedures

Introduction	68
Methods: Telephone Collection v Letter Writing	68
Timing	71
Checks and Balances	72
The Role of the Procedures Manual	73

Chapter 6

Selecting Suitable Chasing Procedures

Introduction

There is still a fundamental fear amongst some legal circles that third party chasing for funds will permanently damage the client's view of the practice. **This should never be the case.** Chasing procedures should aim to meet the needs of the practice taking into consideration the expectations of the client. In short it should be carried out in a professional manner. The following chapter gives guidance for the selection of a suitable chasing cycle and routine which navigates the minefield of client sensitivities.

> ### Objectives
>
> Once you have read this chapter you should be able to:
>
> 1. Choose a suitable method of chasing for your client base
> 2. Set the timing cycle for collection

Methods: Telephone Collection v Letter Writing

Whether letter or telephone is used to chase is entirely up to the needs of the individual practice. However, what is crucial is having a structured chasing cycle, which will make the day to day administration of the debtors ledger easier to control. Some ideas on structuring this chasing cycle are set out below, taking into account client types.

Many practices have both corporate and private clients and although the common denominator is that they all want legal services, they are very different animals when it comes to payment and the differences should be noted when selecting a collection method.

The Differences

The Corporate Client

The corporate client – be it either partnership, limited company or a large plc – will be used to being asked for money from its various creditors. So providing that the credit terms have expired and there is no known query on the bill, no one is going to get upset by payment requests. Corporate clients react better to a telephone call for the first stages of debt collection. The advantage of telephone collection over letter is that is it based on personal contact. If a good rapport can be established between the collector and the person putting forward invoices for bills, the chances of getting paid quickly increase. The telephone call is more versatile than a letter as many items can be raised as the conversation progresses, but a letter remains impersonal and static. Listed below are three advantages of telephone collection over the letter:

1. If the client is to make payment, it can be established on what date that payment will reach the practice. A typical scenario could be:

    On having been told that the bill is to be paid the Collector for the Practice could then say: "How is payment being made: by BACS or Cheque?"
    To which the usual response is "We have a BACS/cheque run on Thursday 25th."
    From which the collector can reasonably suppose that the funds will be with the practice the following week and can look out for them.

2. A telephone call can establish almost immediately whether there is a query which is needs resolving before the bill is paid and requests for copy bills can be satisfied straight away using the fax machine.

3. A call puts the collector in the position whereby if they listen carefully to what is being said they will be able to tell if the client has a genuine query or is purely stalling for time, which could of course mean they have cash flow problems.

Certainly, providing that clients can be actually reached, the telephone is much speedier than a letter, as the collector is not having to sit back and wait for a certain number of days to elapse and waiting to act on a response which may or may not be forthcoming.

If telephone collection is properly carried out, it is a cheap and particularly effective method of credit collection. Certainly, also there is a tendency for Purchase Ledger Departments (especially of large Companies) to ignore or throw away all non essential credit collection letters.

A further advantage of the telephone over the letter is that personal contact reinforces the client relationship with the practice. A dissatisfied client is picked up more quickly and both such a corporate client and those that are satisfied are reminded that the practice is efficient.

The Private Client
It is often better in terms of practicality and sensitivity to approach private clients by letter for payment rather than by telephone. Contacting the private client at home by phone during office hours is often very difficult for a number of reasons, for example they may work full time or part time, go collect the children from schools, go shopping and so on. Very few practices will want to have an evening shift similar to the credit card companies and banks – the costs involved of setting up such an operation would be prohibitive.

The other telephone based option is to ring the client at work to discuss his/her debts. This method is fraught with danger; it will be all too easy to puncture the client's expectations of the practice's respect for their privacy. The collector *has* to ensure that the privacy of the client is maintained at all times. Sometimes switchboards have to be passed to reach a client and the practice should not insist on the collector being put in a position where they might reveal why they rung. Take this a scenario from Slap Dash & Co's Collector:

> Collector to Switchboard: "Could I speak to Mrs Williams please?"
>
> Switchboard: "She's not answering her phone right now, can I take a message?"
>
> Collector to Switchboard. " Yes, could you tell her Mrs Johnson from Slap Dash & Co has rung regarding her outstanding bill for the appearance at the magistrates court for her speeding offence."

Not very professional. At the least this method will do nothing for client confidence in the practice. At worst it will turn them completely against the firm. Remember a satisfied client may tell **some** people about how good you were, the aggrieved client will tell **everybody** how bad you were.

If the client is not available immediately, it is better that the collector rings back, rather than leave a message that a firm of solicitors is wanting a word (for whatever reason). But even if the client is available, the collector must remember that they might not be able to take the call in private to discuss the situation. If the client feels hounded, or has been made to feel embarrassed in front of their colleagues there will be complaints and the practice will gain a poor reputation. There is a very fine line between contacting a client for payment and potentially harassing them.

As a result of these problems with the telephone, letters are usually the best and least potentially offensive method of contact. Most private clients will respond to letters, either by sending a payment, or writing or ringing (when they are able to do so in private) with queries or requests for deferred payments. The telephone can then be used as a last resort using the following rules:

- If calling the workplace seek to speak to the client personally without revealing the matter
- Try to ring back at an agreed time rather than leave a message
- If speaking to a private client (at home or at work) ensure that they can speak freely and in private.

Timing

Having chosen how the clients are going to be approached for collection, a decision has to be made on the timing of the chasing cycle. The choice made will be based on the individual needs of the practice and the resources available. If there is a full time credit controller it will be possible to have a fast revolving cycle based on (say) a seven or 14 days turnaround. If the practice is using part time controllers, a monthly basis may prove more practical. It is important to bear in mind though, that the longer a debt remains outstanding the more difficult it is to collect, and the bigger the increase of lost profit on the bill.

Detailed below are two suggested cycles based on a 14 day turnaround. This two pronged approach to chasing may seem longwinded but it can easily be built into a manual or an automatic credit control process. Any disadvantages relating to the initial time spent setting up the system are easily mitigated by the keeping of the goodwill of the client, and thereby the reputation of the practice with the chances of getting the repeat business that this engenders.

Invoice Age	Suggested Collection Cycle (1) Private Client	Suggested Collection Cycle (2) Corporate Client
31 days Old	Letter 1 & Copy Invoice	Telephone call (1)
45 days old	Letter 2	Telephone Call (2) (if no answer on (1))
53 days	Letter 3	7 day letter if no answer to Tel (2)

Checks & Balances

Once the decision has been made regarding the timing it is necessary to bring in a system of checks and balances in order to eliminate any mistakes when chasing clients for money. This is based on **commonsense and contact.**

Earlier on in the section it was stated that a good credit system was dependent on team work. If the procedures are to progress smoothly (and by that it is meant without offending the client) it is essential that fee earner and credit controller work together. This means that one has to know what the other is doing. The fee earner should let credit control know if the client has put forward a query, and vice versa. If one does not inform the other, the bill will never get paid and the firm might end up taking action it later regrets. Take this scenario from Slap Dash & Co, for example:

> Instant Rich Ltd has a bill for £3000. According to the accounts system they have not paid it despite numerous reminders. Credit Control does not inform the Fee Earner that they are going to sue and duly issues the County Court Summons. Meanwhile the Fee Earner has on his file a cheque for £3000 for which he has acknowledged receipt to the client but not yet paid in.

The moral of the story is that all the facts should be checked prior to taking action that may backfire on the practice and enforce a policy of paying in cheques the same day as they are received!

The Role of the Procedures Manual

All bills should be chaseable, *i.e.* no bills should be put onto a system purely as a target achiever. By making it clear in a Procedures Manual that all bills will be chased at 31 days, without recourse to the fee earner, the firm will effectively limit "fee boosters" from its ledger. In practical terms it is impossible for any but the smallest firm to have the person doing credit control ring up and ask for permission to chase the bills at each and every stage. If this type of policy is implemented the practice will find that cash collections are hindered, as by tradition, fee earners tend to be reticent for anyone other than their secretaries to speak to clients.

However, the credit controller should not be allowed to have carte blanche with the client's account. Lasting damage to the client relationship can be done by the credit controller if the wrong action is taken. What should happen to be both effective and protective of the client/firm relationship is that the credit controller is allowed to chase the client until the seven day letter (or letter before action is issued). This of course is on the basis that there are no known queries. When the seven day letter is due, the fee earner and/or partner in charge of the client should be informed that the client has not paid, and has no excuses for paying that are known. It may be that the fee earner/partner could put some pressure on the client to get payment, *i.e.* threaten not to continue with a case but if not the letter should be authorised and sent. As this letter will be threatening to commence legal action on behalf of the practice, it should be signed by a partner.

It should be remembered that the instigation of legal proceedings against the firm's own client marks the end of that relationship, usually for ever, though it has been known for some clients to come back even after they have been successfully sued! Whether the firm decides to act for the client again is totally dependent on the firm's policy, but it is suggested that if the client is accepted back into the fold, that the old adage, "one bitten twice shy" is followed and the client is asked for funds on account!

Chapter 7

Exposure Levels

Why Do Credit Checks?	76
Protection Of The Saleable Commodity	76
Who Should Do The Checks?	77
The Importance of Adhering to Terms	77
Simple And Free Checks and Balances	78
Paying for Risk Assessment Checks	79
The Ostrich Condition	80

Chapter 7

Exposure Levels

Why Do Credit Checks?

Whenever a person takes out a Hire Purchase Agreement, Mortgage or Credit Card they are checked by the companies providing the loan/finance to verify their credit worthiness. If they are an acceptable risk they are given the loan/finance with the amount provided to them being based on a risk calculation dependent upon assets/income. Essentially they are assessed as to whether they are a good risk to the loan/finance company or whether the company might become exposed to bad debt by dealing with them.

In the commercial world a new customer is usually checked out using bank references and other supplier references, grapevine news or trade magazines. A supplier is not going to allow goods to be made and sent out without knowing whether the customer is able to pay for the goods. The supplier may even ask for the monies on account to ensure that he is not exposed to bad debt.

In both the consumer and the commercial world, lenders do all they can to prevent themselves from becoming exposed to unnecessary bad debt which will have a detrimental affect to their own financial security. They would not consider giving a free loan to a customer without some sense of security. So this begs the question, why do solicitors give their client unsecured loans (in terms of WIP and disbursements) without having done any check to ensure that they will be able to pay them back? This should **Never** be the case.

Protection Of The Saleable Commodity

A practices sells its legal expertise: this is its raw material. As with any commercial business it should protect its stock jealously and ensure that it does not waste any by giving it away for nothing. It should therefore not work for a client who is unable to pay for the services rendered. Just because time and expertise are intangible items, it does mean that they should be treated any differently from a three piece suite in terms of financial protection of the vendor. At least with tangible items the originator may be able to retain title to the goods and resell them. Unfortunately, the same cannot be said for a legal service. Accordingly the checks before supply are *even more* critical.

Practices should therefore help themselves by taking up risk assessment and be systematic in exposure management. They should not simply carry on working for a client who may or may not pay them. The only loser will be the practice.

Who Should Do The Checks?

Ideally the person in charge of the finance section of the practice should carry out any checks relating to risk assessment and they should set the credit limits. This could be the practice manager, accountant or the credit controller who passes a recommendation to the partner in charge of the client.

The limits should be set up at the client level, for the simple reason that a client may have several ongoing cases. The practice must avoid setting limits by matter. Otherwise it is possible to assess the client's limit as £1000 but allow her to have 10 matters all at £999 which together would exceed the desirable limit almost tenfold.

The Importance of Adhering to Terms

It is imperative that these credit limits are adhered to by fee earning staff. Take for example this scenario from Slap Dash & Co:

> The credit controller carries out a credit check on 'Not Very OK Ltd'. It is clear from the check that the company is a bad financial risk, as it has no funds and there is a reduction the shareholders' capital.
>
> The credit controller duly copies the check to the fee earner concerned, with a nil credit rating and a recommendation that funds be obtained on account.
>
> The fee earner proceeds to work for the client but fails to ask for funds on account. He renders a bill for several thousand. This is duly chased, the client giving a variety of stalling tactics to delay payment. Two months after the bill has been rendered the client goes into liquidation and Slap Dash & Co receive (at a much later date) 2 pence in the £ for the debt.

If the fee earner at Slap Dash & Co had heeded the advice of the credit controller then he would have been able to protect the financial exposure of the practice. By ignoring it, he worked for free and the work which he did was of no financial use to the practice whatever.

Simple and Free Checks and Balances

Practices, no matter how small, should check their client base even if it is purely private clients. Simple internal checks can cost nothing and yet save a small fortune in write offs. For example, when doing work for a private client ensure that you have the correct address, and keep a check throughout the file as to where the client lives and where he can be contacted, be it at work or home.

Credit limits should be kept small, and interim billing should be introduced (though this obviously depends upon the type of matter) with work only continued once the interim bills are paid. If the client is selling a property or awaiting settlement for personal injury, divorce etc, an agreement should be made that the bills will be settled out of those funds or be paid by the other side.

With both private clients and corporate clients it is always a good idea for the controller to check what the file is about. If it is fending off an insolvency or a litigation matter which if lost may result in the bankruptcy of the client then arrangements should be made to keep the practice's bills paid on an interim basis. The fee-earner should not risk allowing the costs to rocket, in the hope that it will all work out in the end and the client will be able to pay. This is not being kind to the client, as the practice may end up being the one to push him over the edge financially. Nor is it kind to the cash flow of the practice as the bill will have to written off if it cannot be recovered.

Long Standing Clients

With regard to long standing clients, one free method of checking risk assessment is to check the client's payment history. If the client has always paid on time and never given indication of financial difficulties, then he is probably going to continue for the short term to be so. However, the controller should not get complacent with that client, as financial situations can change quite quickly. If on the other hand, the client has a poor payment history, then arrangements regarding interim billing or payment on account can be made for future work.

Paying for Risk Assessment Checks

It is possible for practices to get information relating to the finances of their corporate clients for a price from several credit agencies, and of course, from Companies House. Details relating to limited companies have to be registered and these can give an insight as to the financial well being of the client. In relation to private clients, checks can be made to confirm their addresses by looking up the electoral roll. The benefit of being able to look up the client via this method is that the fee earner does not have to ask the client embarrassing financial questions or ask for bank references and the client will not know that he has been checked.

There are several agencies which will provide information on line, *i.e.* the system is set up in the practice and therefore always accessible. It is not the purpose of this book to recommend nor give opinions as to which Credit Agency provides the best information for the best price. It is suggested that should a practice feel that it will be of benefit to have the use of an on line system, it should contact a number of the agencies and see what they have to offer. The choice is varied as is the price and quality of the reporting. Some will be able to produce a number of reports varying from a basic check on name and address, or a full report showing the last balance sheet, the directors' names and addresses and also give recommendations with relation to credit limits and give regular status updates in between the current set of accounts and the next date for filing. For example, if the client has a County Court judgment made against them. Some Agencies are able to offer an International Service for those practices with overseas clients. Recommended reading to find the names of the various agencies is *Credit Management* magazine (for contact details see page 130).

The Ostrich Condition

Some legal practices still believe that they are immune to bad debts and that to 'check up' on their clients is not in keeping with their professional status. No practice can afford to stick its head in the sand when it comes to risk assessment, especially in times of recession. It is an accepted fact now that protecting the financial well-being of any company is important. There is no reason why any legal practice should be any different to the rest of the commercial world, after all the idea is to make a profit, not work for nothing.

Achievements

1. It should now be possible to devise and write down the Credit Management Procedures & Polices which will take into account the financial needs of the practice *and* the need for the continuation of client goodwill
2. Decisions about the timing of the chasing cycle and the method to be used based on the client type and the type of risk assessment to be carried out can now be made.

Chapter 8

Setting Up the Administration

Why Bother With Administration?	82
First Step	82
The Second Stage: Recording	86

Chapter 8

Setting Up the Administration

Why Bother With Administration?

In order for the credit control functions to progress smoothly, it is essential that an administration system is set up. This need not be a complex system; in fact the simpler the system to operate the more foolproof it will be. Without some system of administration, the credit controller designate will find it virtually impossible to keep track of what is happening to debtors: who has been chased; who is being sued; who has a query etc. This will of course have a detrimental effect on quality of information filtered into the reports generated for the financial management of the practice. In fact to proceed without such a system would be a bit like getting into a car and driving it down hill knowing that the brakes were not working.

First Step

The first step of any control administration system is to identify the debtors. This can be done in one of two ways, dependent upon the facilities available to the practice. Firstly for the practice with a report generating function (so long as they are accurate reports).

Aged Debtors Reports

An Aged Debt Report needs to be produced from the accounts system. This one report can be the building blocks of an entire administration and credit control function.

The Aged Debt Report should have the following information.

1. **Client Number/Identifier**
   This helps to identify the client on the accounts screen and enables the credit controller to link up other matters on the client's account. This is important if the controller is to be able to make one phone call to the client, or send one letter, rather

than bombarding the client with several calls or letters, which will only serve to irritate.

2   **Client name**
    This is obviously an important method of being able to identify the debtor by name and acts as a checking method when combined with the client number.

3   **Matter Description**
    This is a useful piece of information to have, as it acts not only as a checking mechanism for bills (*i.e.* has the credit controller identified the right bill) but also acts as an information point when ringing the client. It may be that the client has several bills, all for the same amount, but which relate to different matters. It will also serve to alert the controller to matters which need particular care *e.g.* employment matters where the client is contactable at work, or insolvency matters which might need priority.

4   **Bill Number**
    This is an essential identification: the credit controller needs to know which particular bill is outstanding on a matter.

5   **Bill Date**
    This is required as it is the data on which the Aged Debt is based.

6   **Bill Amount Due/Amount Outstanding**
    The amount which is currently outstanding should be put onto the Aged Debt Report, not the original amount of the bill, as this may only lead to confusion. It will often be useful to run the Aged Debt Report sorting by size so that (as the Pareto principle would have it) the 20% of accounts outstanding that have 80% of the value are prioritised.

7   **Client Account Balance**
    This is extremely useful when a credit controller is basing the chasing on the Aged Debt, as it lets them know that there are funds held on the client account which may be for allocation against the bill.

A Word Of Warning
The Aged Debtors Report whilst being the basis on which the credit controller works should always be verified by a look at the accounts screen, due to time lapses in inputting from cashiers.

The Calendar Method for Identifying Debtors

If a practice is unable to produce an accurate Aged Debtors Reports, the most simple method of being able to see what is outstanding is for the credit controller to set up a calendar system. This entails being given a *copy* set of bills – not the originals – each month (preferably on a daily basis as they are inputted). These are then filed in a ordinary lever arch file, with dividers of 1–31. Each divider corresponds to the day the bill was raised. Thus if a bill was raised on 1st January, it would be put in the divider numbered one, bills raised on 2nd January would be put in the divider number two and so on until coming to the end of the month.

Only one binder is necessary as the credit controller will be pulling out current chasing bills. Thus if it is February 1st, the controller would go to the number one divider and pull out all the bills to check for payment. Those bills which were paid would be thrown away and the others that required chasing would be filed into the chasing files (see later in this chapter). This would obviously leave the divider numbered one free for the new bills of February to be placed, and this would continue on daily basis.

Once the bill has been taken out of the bills file and an action taken, *e.g.* a letter raised or a call made, the credit controller should then use a diary to record when the next action should be taken. So for example a letter sent on 1st February for a 1st January bill, would have its next action date on 7 February (on a 7 day chasing cycle). This could be put in the diary as "Instant Rich Co Ltd, bill no 12345, phone call (or letter 2). The credit controller should look at the diary every day to see what action needs to be taken on what bills. The above is a very simple and cost effective method for a manual credit control system, with the advantage that staff turnover or changes in personnel should not interrupt the collection of cash provided that the details are recorded in systematically and correctly.

Setting Up the Administration 85

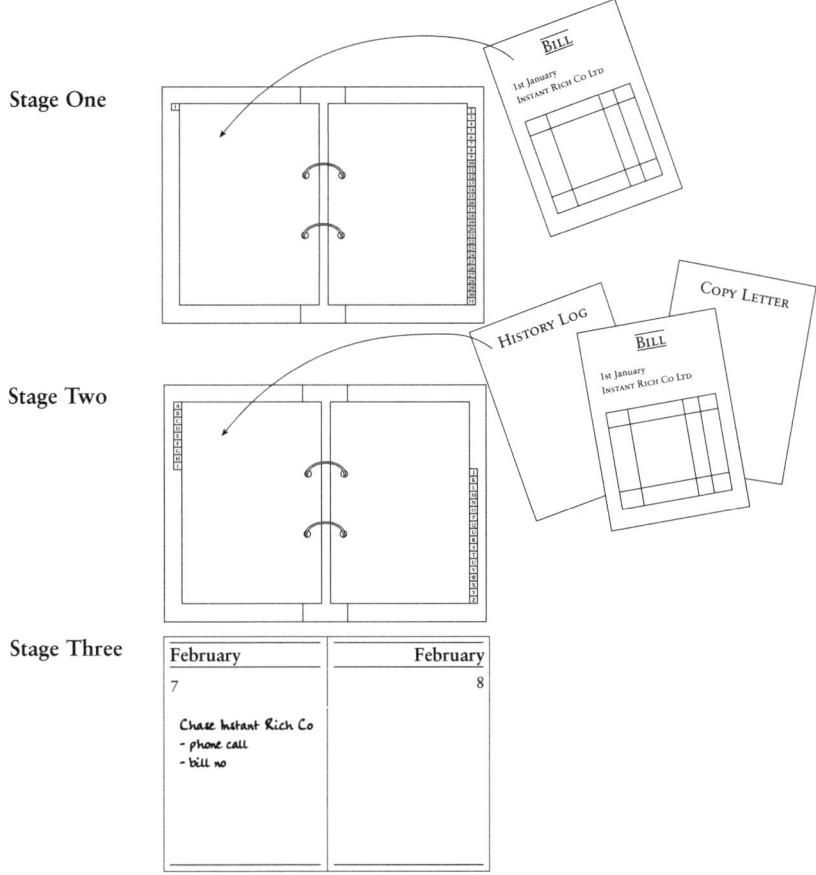

Stage One

Stage Two

Stage Three

Figure 4: The calendar method

Automatic Systems: First Steps

If the practice has an automatic chasing system, neither the Aged Debt nor the calendar method is necessary, as the system will monitor and diarise chasing for the credit controller. Literally all the credit controller will have to do is follow the instructions, whether it is time to send a letter, make a phone call or check that an instalment payment has come in. Letters will be run off automatically, but it is a good idea for the sake of good client relations to check that the correct billing address has been used and the amount is correct. No system is fool proof and inputters make mistakes. Moreover, if a client has sent in a cheque the day before or that morning it may not have been allocated, when the letter run was sent.

The Second Stage: Recording

Why Have a History Section?

It should never be the case that a bill is paid and the client forgotten about until next time. It is important that a relationship between the credit controller and the client is built up and this can be helped by the use of history logs, which will record contact addresses, telephone and fax number and names of relevant parties. It is a lot easier and more time effective if when the client has another bill, the credit controller can fetch out a log detailing all the information they will need, rather than having to build it up every time the client has a new bill.

However, history logs are not just useful from a contact point of view. They also, if accurately filled out, help the credit controller establish the payment pattern of the client and provide a good risk indicator, which can be useful to know when chasing debts or deciding on credit limits for the client. For example, a client may be a very good payer, but one day fails to keep to the pattern over a particular bill. This will indicate to the credit controller, not that the client has suddenly turned into a bad payer, but rather that there is a problem with that one bill. With this insight the credit controller can then speak or write to the client, addressing their concern that the bill may have a query and if so can they help by either addressing the problem direct or speaking to the fee earner concerned. This is a much more positive, proactive and professional approach, than just assuming that the client is now a bad payer and demanding payment, which if there is a query will only serve to annoy the client and damage the relationship with the client.

On the other hand if the client is habitual bad payer, it can be suggested to the fee earner that in future monies should be paid on account if undertaking any further work. This will of course protect the practice's exposure to the client.

Keeping history logs is also a help when either a change over in staff occurs, whether through holiday cover or sickness or permanent replacement. If the new credit controller is given a set of full and accurate history logs, they will be able to pick up the chasing much quicker than having to start literally from scratch again. The latter course obviously carries the danger of upsetting the client, if he is being chased and he has a genuine and ongoing query.

Automatic Systems

History Logs: Client or Bill Level?

Some automatic systems default automatically to chase and record at bill level, which is fine until the bill is paid, and then all the information entered at the bill level is wiped off as the bill is no longer registrable on the system. The history log should always be kept at *client* level, as this is really the easiest method to link all a particular client's matter and bills together. This should be done irrespective of whether the practice has a manual credit control system or an automatic system. None of the benefits outlined above would accrue to the practice without client level history.

Information to be Put onto the Customer Query Logs

- Date and details of phone calls should always be accurately recorded. Information as to who said what to whom and on what date is vitally important. Failure to do this can result in a chaotic and unprofessional follow up call, where the credit controller cannot remember who promised payment or on what date they said the cheque had been sent. It is much better and more professional to be able to contact the same person, or somebody else and say that

    "when we spoke (or "when I spoke to John Johnstone") on Monday the 14th you (he) said that a cheque was to be sent out first class that night, but as yet we haven't received it."

    This way the credit controller is able to provide the potential payer with all the facts they are likely to need to ensure that they are able to look into the matter, whilst the credit controller is on the phone. A woolly conversation, where the credit controller does not know to whom they have spoken or dates of promises, allows the client, to be able to say things, like

    "I'll look it up and get back to you". Which of course they won't.

    Thus the credit controller has allowed the client to extend his credit further.

- If the client is paying by instalments, this should be logged. The dates of when payments are received and the new balance of the bill should be entered onto the log, so that the credit controller is in no doubt at any point as to what is owed, and when the last instalment was paid, and the next is due.

- Copies of letters sent and received should also be kept on the customer log. It may be that the client has written in with a reason why they won't pay the bill, and this needs to be kept on record.

- Also any internal communications should be documented and kept. *i.e.* memos or telephone calls with fee earners.

- Once the bill is paid the hard copy information (*i.e.* copy letters from the credit controller or client or memos) can be placed with the remittance slip and archived, so that whilst it is kept for future reference should it ever be needed, it does not clutter up the chasing files with information which is not relevant to current matters in hand.

Some information, such as "letter 1 sent on 12 June" will be entered onto the history log by the system itself, and only those actions outside the collection package's scope, such as telephone conversations or special non chasing sequence letters will need to be entered up onto the client history. Hard copies of information such as letters, memos, e-mails obviously need to be kept, but can only be referred to as having been received or gone out on the recording system. The best solution for ' spare paperwork' of this nature is to enter on the automatic log that an item has been received or sent out and give it a location key, *i.e.* where the credit controller has put the item. This can be either in a client file specifically set up for that client, or in a general correspondence file such as an A–Z concertina file under the appropriate initial for the client.

Manual Chasing

Records for a manual chasing system should be set up in a series of files using an alphabetic system, *i.e.* the history logs are filed in alphabetical order. This is the easiest way of setting up a system, as most practices give their client's numbers as identifiers and there is no way that anybody is going to be able to remember every number ever issued to every client. It is much easier to have a sort of telephone directory system, where Mr Alexander's history log is put in the A file, and Mr Nicholas's history log is placed in the N file. This is virtually a foolproof system, and theoretically, anybody should be able to find the history log they want straight away.

"Problem" Clients

Should the practice have a lot of clients paying by instalments, it may be an idea to set up a special instalments file, which would make it simpler for the credit controller to monitor, ideally on a weekly basis. This could be just one file or two (depending on the number of logs) divided using A–Z dividers.

This could also be done for clients being sued by the practice or for clients with queries.

The idea being that these three types of "problem" client are kept out of the way of the main stream chasing A–Z files, and yet are not able to be forgotten or ignored.

Sample Recording Systems

The history log for the manual system should be made of card, as it is going to (depending on the length of the relationship with the client) be used for quite some time. It should also be double sided to keep as much of the history together. A suggested format for the log is detailed below. Whilst this can be changed to suit the individual house style of practices, it should be noted that the information section should be included if the manual system is to work efficiently.

SLAP DASH & CO
COLLECTIONS HISTORY LOG

NAME OF CLIENT _____

CLIENT NO _____

ADDRESS _____

_____

_____

TEL NO _____ FAX NO _____

CONTACT NAME _____

Additional Information _____

DATE OF ACTION	DETAILS	FOLLOW UP DATE

Remittance Advices

One final administration system to set up is the filing away of remittance advices. These may be required at some later date to prove payment. These should be kept in a file in date order. An ordinary lever arch file, with 1–31 dividers will do for the current month. Once the credit controller is onto a new month, the advices should put into a large envelope, clearly marked, *e.g.* 'Remittance Advices 1 January 1998 – 31 January 1998' and stored.

An Optional But Useful Log To Have

Alongside the history logs, the credit controller will find it useful to have a one page aide memoir logs for either payment promises or queries. Nobody can be expected to remember all the clients that have promised payment next week, but it is information which may be needed on an immediate basis by either a fee earner waiting to pay out a disbursement on a particular matter, or an accountant wanting a general picture of the funds expected to come in. It will also enable the credit controller to keep a track of non-appearing payments.

The log should be simple in design and easy to fill out. Information should be entered as soon as the promise is made. The log will probably be entirely made up of telephone promises as it unlikely that a client will write in and let the credit controller know the date of the cheque run.

If the client has a query the date of the query can be logged and by whom the query is being actioned. As clients have been known to use the excuse of one bill in query to prevent payment of the rest of their account, it is essential that queries are dealt with as speedily as possible. By having the log the credit controller will be able to chase up the person dealing with the query more easily and speedily from the one sheet log than going through the entire A–Z collections files.

PAYMENT PROMISE/QUERY LOG SHEET

DATE	CLIENT NAME & NO	QUERY/DEALT WITH BY	PAYMENT PROMISE DATE	AMOUNT	SATISFIED

Achievements

1. The firm will now be in position to set up or review an administration system on which the credit controller can chase in an effective and controlled manner.

Chapter 9

Collection Techniques

The Options	96
The Letter	97
To Write or to Ring?	97
Getting The Right Message Across	98
Sample Letters	101
Telephone Collection	108
Statements: are they an Effective Method?	113

Chapter 9

Collection Techniques

Whereas the last four chapters have been dealing with the theory behind the setting up of a Credit Management System, the next two chapters deal with the practicalities of chasing monies *i.e.* the collection techniques available to the Law Firm and who should use them.

The Options

As has been said, there are two main methods of chasing available to any law firm, regardless of size or client base: the letter and the telephone call. Each method has its advantages and disadvantages and as discussed in Chapter 6, one method may be more suitable than the other in relation to certain client types.

It may be possible to operate more by telephone than letter chasing in a larger or more corporate based firm than in a smaller or purely private client based firm, but it is doubtful if any firm could get by totally excluding one method. At some point the corporate client will have to be written to and the private client will have to be spoken to.

There is one further method of collection open to the firm: statements. These are becoming more widely used by firms for both their corporate clients and private clients. Whether this is an option will depend on the resources available to you, both in terms of manpower and accounts systems. The pros and cons of sending statements will be discussed later on in the chapter.

It is vital to remember that any chasing that is carried out, by any of the three methods, has to be proactive, positive and professional. It is no good chasing bills that have already been paid, or upsetting the client by a clumsy or aggressive approach, which will only backfire onto the practice. Occasionally when the client says the cheque is in the post it will be the truth, but if the credit controller takes the stance that the client is lying and makes it clear to the client that they think that is the case, and the cheque then turns up, the chances are that the client will be sufficiently insulted not to come back to the practice again.

Collection Techniques

Objectives

1. To enable the production of a set of effective collection letters for your firm
2. To assist the controller to make effective use of the telephone
3. To help with the decision whether statements are a viable option for your firm

Credit control is the last point of contact with the client: make it count both monetarily *and* in terms of good client relations.

The Letter

The letter has two purposes in the collections field. It can:

1. Serve as a gentle reminder to the client, to pay the bill, or:
2. Inform the client that if the bill is not paid proceedings will be issued in order to recover costs.

To Write or to Ring?

It was discussed in Chapter 6 whether letters were the right medium to chase clients for money. Whilst it is generally accepted that the letter is not a particularly effective method of collection (due to factors of elapsed time between receipt and answer, and the fact that they are easy to ignore or pretend that they have never been received), no firm will find that it is able to get by without ever having to send a single letter to a client regarding outstanding accounts. Even if the firm has a 100% corporate base, it would be highly unlikely that chasing could be done solely via the telephone. For example, some of the smaller companies or partnerships may only have a part time accounts person. They may during office hours just use an answer phone whilst they are not in their offices. Very few companies will ring back in relation to a message requesting payment! Certainly, notice of intention to take legal action to recover a debt, *must* be done by letter. For the firm who is either wholly or partially based on private client work, the letter may be the only acceptable medium for chasing.

Getting The Right Message Across

It is imperative that any letters sent to the client, get their message across loud and clear, whilst at the same time take into consideration the client relationship. To that end the letters should be polite, concise but firm. However, a practice should not send out letters which allow the client to form the opinion that they are grovelling for money, or desperate for money.

There are two basic concepts to remember when devising the chasing letter:

> a) the client is enjoying a free loan from the firm, i.e. the client is now at the stage where he is costing the firm money in lost interest.
> b) the firm will want (in most circumstances) a long term relationship with the client.

The Main Body Of The Letter

Any letter sent to the client should show that the firm is professional right down to its credit chasing procedures. (Remember the three P's: Proactive, Positive Professional.) The letter should include the following features:

1 **It should be clearly addressed to the person responsible for the payment of the bill**
 Sometimes bills are payable by a third party, and it is important that the chasing letter is sent to the right party, in the interests of both the client relationship, and the professional reputation of the firm. Remember in Chapter 5 that the credit controller has follow the three P's (Proactive, Positive & Professional). The credit controller, should look out a copy of the bill and see whether it is payable by the actual client or a third party. A third party bill should have the name and address of the payer on it, as well as the client's name.

Alternatively if the bill is to be paid by the client the letters should be addressed to the person who has authorised the work to be done. Sending letters for the attention of the Purchase Ledger Department can be a waste of time, unless the controller is able to reference the letter back to the original authoriser of the work.

2. **The letter should be concise polite but firm and factual**
Nobody is going to spend time reading a letter resembling War & Peace, which simply requests payment. A few lines of short and simple words will do nicely. The letter should be polite as it needs to be indicative of the firm and the way the firm views its clients, but it should not be a grovelling letter: after all it is the firm's money of which the client is making use. The client has to be persuaded to part with the funds but if there is a genuine problem, a clumsily worded request can backfire.

3. **Use all client references**
Letters requesting payment should be as helpful to the client as possible. Bear in mind that the firm will not be the client's only debtor. For that matter the firm may have several on-going cases for a particular client, covering either the one area or even different departments within that area or different areas all together, which may have individual accounting sections. By putting the all the necessary client references on the chasing letter the client is provided with information to tie up his files with the request for payment. This also has the added advantage of by-passing a traditional method of delaying payment – the client stating that he cannot tie up his paperwork until the controller comes up with a reference!

4. **Contain the practice's references and the credit controller's name**
This is really a self help option for the credit controller for ease of reference should the client ring. The client has the opportunity to speak directly to an named individual, rather than an anonymous person and is therefore not being passed around from person to person in the accounts office, each time having to explain why he is ringing. By having the practice's reference on the letter, the credit controller has an identification point and should easily find the accounts details either on the screen or in the filing system. This gives an appearance of a smooth and professional operation as the client is not asked to hang on for

ages whilst the credit controller tries to find the client's details using a search facility based on the client's name. If the client is agitated with the letter or the account in general waiting for the credit controller to get their act together will only serve to irritate further and damage the client relationship.

5   **Letters should reflect an accurate account picture**
    Always check that the amount requested in the letter is the amount which is owed. Nothing looks more unprofessional and is more likely to annoy a client than by requesting the wrong amount of money, especially if requesting too much money. Of course the other side of the coin is, that if too little is requested, the client may take the opportunity to pay the reduced sum, and it will be very difficult to persuade the client to part with the remainder once you have established the wrong figure in writing.

6   **Put in a date by which payment should be made**
    Setting an actual date for a payment *i.e.* 'Tuesday 7 January 199x' is a better method than stating a passage of time, *e.g.* '7 days' as it leaves no room for mis-interpretation as to when the 7 days are up.

The Escalation Technique

It is advisable when devising the chasing letters that as the debt gets older the letters get firmer. So, in effect:

- the first letter is a gentle reminder in case the client has 'forgotten, or 'overlooked' payment and allows for the assumption of a problem;
- the second gives a set time for payment and assumes there is no problem; and
- the third informs the client that if payment is not forthcoming by a certain date, proceedings will be issued without further recourse.

There is little point in sending out letter after letter requesting payment. Three letters give the client more than enough time to get their act together and either pay the bill or reveal the query. The reluctant paying client will be more than happy with a situation whereby the firm sends letter after letter of gentle pleadings for funds. The only party which will lose out will be the firm, which will run up a large and unnecessary stationery and postage bill. The client will merely fill up his waste basket!

Write It And Mean It

There is little point in sending out a Letter before Action, if there is no intention of carrying out the threat. It may work the first time, but clients soon get used to the idea that these are sent out but mean very little in real terms. It is like having a guard dog without teeth: purposeless.

Non Standard Letters

Letters outside those of the main chasing cycle will need to be used from time to time. The more common ones relate to part payments, acceptance of instalment payments or revocation of instalment facilities when instalments payments have failed to materialise! It is a good idea to have a stock of pre-prepared non-standard chasers in order to save time in drafting new ones, every time this type of event occurs.

Sample Letters

Below are suggested formats for the body of the letters for both the main chasing cycle and the non standard letters. These are only a guide to what could be written, and obviously each individual practice will have its own house style and may prefer to substitute different wording. However, in essence the letters should remain fairly standard.

Letter 1 – A polite, gentle reminder to the client

This may be accompanied by a copy of the invoice – this is optional for individual practices, but a plus side to doing this is that the client cannot request a copy and thereby delay payment further. The amount outstanding and the due payment date should be highlighted to ensure they cannot be missed.

Client's name and details

RE Invoice No 211456 – Personal Injury Claim

We note from our records that the above invoice is outstanding in the sum of £1263.26. We enclose a copy of the invoice for your ease of reference.

Should you have any queries relating to this invoice please let us know immediately.

Alternatively, we look forward to receiving payment no later than **THURSDAY 19 FEBRUARY**.

Yours sincerely

Name of Credit Controller (Ext No)
Name of Practice

CL1 – Gentle reminder

Letter 2 – A firmer reminder

A good place to remind the client that interest may be charged on the debt and that the firm's patience is wearing thin.

Client's name and details

RE Invoice No 211456 – Personal Injury Claim

Further to our previous letter dated 12th February regarding the above numbered bill for £1263.26, we note that to date we have had no response from you.

We must now ask that you give this matter your immediate attention and make payment by **THURSDAY 26 FEBRUARY.**

Please note that our terms are 30 days from the bill date, and that we reserve the right to impose interest on the balance outstanding form the date of the bill to the date of payment.

Yours sincerely

Name of Credit Controller (Ext No)
Name of Practice

CL2 – Firmer reminder

Letter 3 – Letter Before Action

This has to be very clear, and the client has to be left in no doubt that proceedings will be instigated if the payment is not made. It should also have a different layout than the other two letters, so that it stands out from the regular chasers.

Client's name and details

OVERDUE ACCOUNT – £1263.26

Your account is now seriously overdue.

Should we not receive payment by **THURSDAY 5 MARCH** we shall issue proceedings against you for the full recovery of the debt plus interest and costs without further notice to you.

Yours sincerely

Name of Credit Controller (Ext No) or Partner
Name of Practice

CL3 – Letter Before Action

Acceptance of Instalments Letter

It is of benefit to the practice if the client can be persuaded to use a Standing Order Mandate or a Direct Debit for instalment payments rather than rely on the client to remember each month to send a payment in. In the letter of acceptance a Mandate/Direct Debit form can be included if the client has agreed to pay using either or these methods.

Client's name and details

RE Invoice No 211456 – Personal Injury Claim – £1263.26

Further to your letter/telephone call. We confirm that we shall accept instalment payments against the above account.

The terms of which are as follows:

Payment	£****
Due Date	** of each month
Commencement Date	************
Finishing Date	************
Payment Method Direct	Debit/Cheque/ Standing Order *

We enclose a standing Order Mandate for you to complete and return to us*

We enclose a Direct Debit Instruction to be rendered to your bank.*

Please ensure that all payments are received by the due date as agreed. If not we will be forced to withdraw the instalment facility whereupon the full balance outstanding of the account will become immediately due and payable.

Yours sincerely

Name of Credit Controller (Ext No)
Name of Practice

---

* Fill in or delete from the main body of the letter depending on the arrangement made with the client. There is no point sending a Standing Order Form, if the client has said they would prefer to pay by cheque.

Withdrawal of Instalments Letter

If the client does not keep up their instalment payments, the whole bill should become due immediately. Often the threat of this will spur the client on to continue the regular payment. However, only let the client get away with non payment once, or it will become a habit. One problem to be aware of when accepting instalments is that when the bill is brought down to a level where it is not cost effective to issue proceedings, the client may attempt to cease payment all together and remainder of the debt will end up being written off.

Client's name and details

RE Invoice No 211456 – Personal Injury Claim – £1263.26

We note from our records that your instalment payment is overdue. Please bring your account up to date without delay to avoid the facility being withdrawn, thus rendering the whole outstanding balance due and payable.

Yours sincerely

Name of Credit Controller (Ext No)
Name of Practice

CL5 – Withdrawal of Instalments

Part Payment Letter

Clients occasionally send in the wrong amounts or part pay the bills. It should always be made clear to the client that the remainder of the bill is still owed. (Check first though, that a credit note is not due to the client, which accounts for the shortfall in payment or that there is not another party responsible for part of the bill.)

Client's name and details

RE Invoice No 211456 – Personal Injury Claim – £1263.26

We thank you for your payment of £1000.00 in part payment of the above account.

We look forward to receiving the balance of the account £263.26 no later than **THURSDAY 19 FEBRUARY**.

Yours sincerely

Name of Credit Controller (Ext No)
Name of Practice

CL6 – Part payments

All these letters should be set up onto a word processor using mailmerge or set up on the automatic chasing system, to enable the credit controller to be able to use the same letters over and over again without the need for re-typing the main body. This will save time enabling the credit controller to contact more clients.

Keeping Ahead Of The Client

It is very easy for the client to get used to seeing the same letters month in month out and it is recommended that the wording or the font is changed every six months so that the client has to at least look twice at what has been sent.

Telephone Collection

Collection via the telephone is generally considered to be the most effective of the collection techniques, as it puts the collectors in direct and immediate communication with the debtor. If handled badly it is also the most potentially damaging of the collection methods in respect of the client relationship. With experience the credit controller should be able to establish if there is a genuine query on the account or if the client is just playing for time. The credit controller may also be able to gauge from the conversations as to whether the client is in financial difficulties which will have an effect on whether the practice gets payment at all.

Preparing For The Call

Successful and non-stressful telephone collections (for both the collector and the client) can only be carried out if the credit controller is fully prepared, and by this it is meant that they have all the necessary information to hand. It will not always be the case that the credit controller is the one doing the phoning. Sometimes the client may phone the collector in response to a letter or if they have dealt with the collector before and feel that the controller will be able to deal with their query. (Clients sometimes will use credit control to approach the fee earners for them, because credit control will not be on chargeable time!) This is why accurate and up to date records need to be kept. There is nothing worse for a client than having to hang on the phone (especially if credit control have telephoned them) whilst the controller goes of to search out the information. It gives the impression of lack of professionalism.

The basic information which should be taken into account before making a call is:

1. Details of *all* the accounts you wish to speak to that client about. Remember a client may have more than one invoice and will not appreciate several phone calls. One call is more than enough for most clients.

2. Make sure that it is the right client you are ringing for payment and check for any invoices which may be payable by a third party.

3   Check whether the matter is private and confidential, in which case contact the person who has authorised the matter (this information should be on the bill but if not the fee earner should supply it). Do not tell third parties *i.e.* accounts departments what the issue is about: keep it general *i.e.* general legal matters, or employment law advice.

4   Check that there are no outstanding queries on the accounts.

5   Check that any client to office transfers which should have been done have been.

6   Know the exact amount of money owed.

7   Have the firm's bank details to hand, should your client wish to pay by BACS.

Timing The Call

Unlike letters which can be typed up anytime during the day, a telephone call has to be made at specific times in order for contact to be made and for that contact to be productive. Calls are usually most effective between the hours of 9:30 to 12:00 and 2:00 to 4:30. Any earlier than 9:30 and the chances are that the post will not be opened, computers will not be operating at the clients or the purchase ledger people will not be settled into their daily routines. Any later than 4:30 and the computer systems maybe doing back ups, or the purchase ledger people are sorting their own internal administration out. If the credit controller does call, the person at the other end may be unable or unwilling to look out your invoice until the next day. The hours of 12 to 2:00 are obviously out because of lunch breaks.

Further restrictions on when the credit controller is able to contact a client will depend on the client's own arrangements. Often account departments will not take calls at certain time of the day and the credit controller will have to get to know when the client is contactable.

Making The Call

The point of the telephone call is two fold:

1. To establish whether there is anything delaying payment.

   If so all details of the client's query should be logged and copied to the appropriate person for remedial action. The query should be sorted in as short a time as possible. The credit controller can then ring up the client and ask for payment to be sent.

2. To establish when payment will be forthcoming.

Establishing Relationships Between Credit Controller & Client

If possible (and contacts with regular clients will be built up in time) the credit controller should be able to direct their phone call to a specific person who will be able to either authorise payment themselves, or contact someone who can. Good relationships which are built up between credit controller and client can pay dividends with regard to getting preferential treatment in the cheque runs. A few seconds of friendly chat can go a long way in establishing a relationship, rather than a standard and static request for funds each time.

Sorting Out The Wheat From The Chaff – Delaying Tactics Or Genuine Queries?

During the course of telephone collections the credit controller will come across a wide variety of delaying tactics. Some of these will be easy to detect and to overcome some will not. It is essential that the credit controller always keeps control of themselves over the telephone, never pre-judging the client, or letting their own views on the situation show through. Keeping cool is an essential element of the job even if the client has asked for the same invoice five times!

Some of the most common excuses, such as

> "The cheque is in the post"
> "We haven't had an invoice"
> "There is query relating to the invoice"

or the classic one which solicitors will have heard many times "the fees are outrageous, the bill is much more than we were expecting"

can have standard retorts to them, which will enable the credit controller to ascertain whether the client is telling the truth or merely bluffing for extra time.

Is the Cheque in the Post?
The first thing that should be remembered is that the client is always right (until proven wrong). It may be that the client has sent the cheque in the post. It is quite acceptable to ask what day it was sent, to whom it was addressed, and whether it has been cashed. The emphasis at this stage should be that the credit controller believes the client and will go out of their way to look for the cheque at their end. This then gives a room for manoeuvre for either party: either the client can get a cheque out, or the credit controller can find the cheque and neither party has lost face.

If found, the credit controller can ring to confirm to the client that they have received the cheque. If not found, the credit controller can ring the client back to ask if the cheque has been cashed, and if not whether they would mind re-issuing the cheque as it has gone missing. This may seem a longwinded approach, but protecting the client care relationship is paramount, and few (if any) clients will use the excuse twice (for the same invoice).

If however, the credit controller makes it clear that they do not believe the client there may be no escaping the following scenario.

> Slap Dash & Co's credit controller rings a client for an outstanding bill. He is told that it was sent out the previous week. The credit controller makes it clear that they do not believe the client and asks that another payment be made immediately failing which they will issue begin charging interest. The client sends a cheque immediately, which the credit controller banks, thinking that they had been right and the client had not paid.
>
> Later that morning the client rings the credit controller. They have been sent their original cheque back with a letter stating that they could not allocate the cheque and could they have more references. The result? The client who had hitherto been satisfied by the performance of the practice was now angry, feeling that he had been cheated. The credit controller was left in the embarrassing position of having to apologise profusely to the client.

No Invoice?
Clients may use the excuse of "not having received the invoice". This may be true. The best approach is to send one to a named individual by fax or post or both. Ring to confirm that they have received the invoice and proceed to chase from there. If the client comes back again stating they have not got the invoice, the credit controller can remind them that it was sent to Helen on Monday 28 and she confirmed receipt. This leaves them little room for manoeuvre – if they delay using a different excuse, it should be obvious to the credit controller that the client is playing the delaying game.

Is the Invoice *Really* Correct?
The best approach to take with a client who maintains there is query, or that the bill is not in line with agreed fees is to take the approach that the client *may* be telling the truth, be sympathetic, and let the client know that the query will be relayed immediately to the fee earner concerned. By doing this the client is aware that internal communications are taking place, so they know that if the query is not genuine, or that a bill has been agreed, you will find out and come back to them for payment, sooner rather than later.

Never agree with the client regarding a fee earner problem, or agree with their criticism with the amount of the bill. This is unprofessional. Merely state that their problem will be forwarded on to so and so and that they will be contacting the client direct.

What To Do If The Client Is Unavailable

By keeping a short telephone log the credit controller can make their job easier and more streamlined. The client will not always be available on the first call, but that does not mean that they should be left until the credit controller's next time through the files, which may be a week later or more. Rather the credit controller should ascertain (wherever possible) when the client will be available to take the calls. This should be noted on the log, which can be scanned quickly by the credit controller on an hourly or daily basis and the client rung at the appropriate time.

Of course there will be some clients who are never available. All the credit controller can do is try to contact the client, and if this fails and time is passing, the credit controller should pass the debt to the fee earner. It is very unlikely that the client will not speak to his lawyer, as it may be concerning the case! They are unlikely to guess that the fee earner is interested in the status of the bill (although of course this should always be the case!).

Telephone calls can be both a help and hazard for the credit controller of the legal practice. However, if due consideration is given to the above, the pitfalls of direct communication should be able to be avoided leaving a happy and healthy credit controller/client relationship to develop. By way of a bonus, this will also lead to the smoother relationship between credit controller and fee earner who will feel more inclined to let the credit controller 'loose' on his clients.

Statements: are they an Effective Method?

The third method of chasing is by statements. Practices both large and small are increasingly using the statement as a method of gently reminding the client of his obligation. Whilst generally regarded as the least effective of the chasing methods, having a tendency to end life in the waste basket...there are some clients who will only pay on production of a statement. Even if the practice is not going to send out a general statement run, it is a wise precaution to ascertain which of the clients have this arrangement and send out 'one off' statements to facilitate payment. This data can be collected through the historic logs, as when the first bill is not paid using this reason, the client can be moved to a separate statement reminder batch. Such clients will rarely bend to the practice's way of working if this is genuinely their procedure.

The Pros And Cons Of The Statement Run

Pros

1. The client is able to ascertain his indebtedness at a glance.
2. The client can see whether there are any invoices missing.
3. The statement can be sent out to both private clients and corporate clients alike.

Cons

1. The client may get fed up of paperwork, especially if a letter run has just gone out, so in effect he gets reminded twice.
2. There can be problems if the bill is payable by a third party, as this will need entering onto the accounts system on a special statement code so that the original client does not get reminded.
3. If there is a large client base, it is expensive in terms of stationery and postage. It can also be time consuming for the credit controller, who will have to sort through the statements to check that they have the correct details, and will then have to fold and envelope them.

What Should A Statement Look Like?

If a practice decides that statements are a suitable method for chasing, then it should ensure that the statements sent out are as effective as possible. The idea is to remind the client:

- how much he owes,
- how long he has owed it, and
- to whom he owes it.

An example of a statement is shown below. Obviously each practice can have its own individual house style, and the paper that the statement is printed on (be it A4 or A3) will depend on the accounts

STATEMENT

SLAP DASH & CO.
14, PARKSTONE AVE
LEEDS LS8 1DD

Instant Rich Ltd.
59–87 Dobb Industrial Estate
New Walklands
West Yorkshire

Client No: 222:178:11

VAT INFO.

DATE: 28/2/98

Date	Bill No.		Bill amount	Amount Due
30/1/98	17952I	Wills	50.00	50.00
			Total Due	

Current	30–60	60–90	180+
50.00	–	–	–

SLAP DASH & CO.
14, PARKSTONE AVE, LEEDS, LS8 1DD

REMITTANCE ADVICE

Instant Rich Ltd.
59–87 Dobb Industrial Estate
New Walklands
West Yorkshire

Client No: 222:178:11   DATE: 28/2/98

Date	Bill No.	£
30/1/98	179321	50.00
	Total Due	50.00

S1: Statement

system and printers available. However, certain basic points of information should always be included and these are:

> 1 The Client's Name and Number
> 2 Client Address
> 3 A clear list of all the outstanding invoices and to what they relate
> 4 An ageing band showing the various ages of the outstanding invoices
> 5 A payment slip which can be torn off and returned with payment or a second copy which can be sent back
> 6 The practice's details so that the client knows where to send the payments (this is particularly important if the bill is payable by a third party

Timing Of The Statement Run

When the statement run is to be sent out is up to the individual practice. The second week of the month is probably the best time to send out a statement run as there is plenty of time then for the client to be able to put the due bills on that month's cheque run, which is usually run during the last week of the month. Month end is probably not the ideal time to send out a statement run due to the fact that accounts personnel are too busy closing ledgers and balancing to be bothered looking at statements.

> ### *Achievements*
>
> 1 It should now be possible to create a set of letters suitable to the chasing cycle and house style of the practice
> 2 Controllers should now be able to make effective and positive use of telephone collection methods without having a detrimental effect to the client relationship.
> 3 How to use statements effectively and appropriately should now be clear.

Chapter 10

Selection And Training Of Personnel

The Selection Process 119
Practical Training – For The Credit Controller 122
Inter Departmental Training 126
Outside Training 129

Chapter 10

Selection And Training Of Personnel

By now you should be able to set up a credit management system suitable for your own practice. All that is needed now is the staff to carry it out.

The selection and training of a credit controller should be dealt with as meticulously as the selection of any other member of the practice, be it fee earning or support staff. Credit controllers are often the last point of contact with the client and the way in which they deal with that client can be pivotal in whether or not the client has a long term relationship with the practice.

The credit controller should be an ambassador for the practice. The way in which they carry out their work, should be as professional, proactive and positive as any member of staff within the practice.

However, if credit control is to be successful, it cannot work in isolation or independently from the rest of the practice. It needs the co-operation of both fee earning and support staff. As seen in the diagram below credit control touches on several of groups of personnel within a practice.

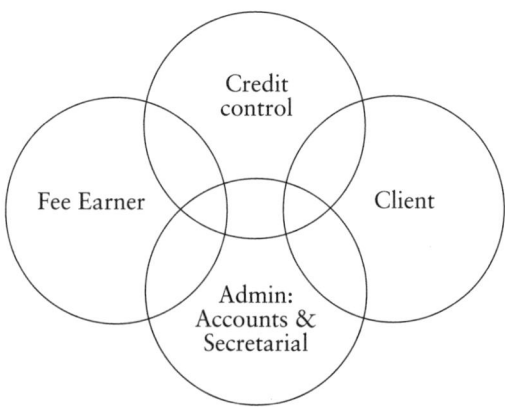

Figure 5: Interdepartmental links with credit control

To this end firms, regardless of size, should provide basic training *for all in the firm* on the functions and practices of credit control. CLT's video and disk package will enable this process to be done by anyone with a basic knowledge. The negative image, which all too often accompanies credit control and is left to fester should be dispelled. Instead an era of communication, co-operation and understanding should be introduced.

> ### Objectives
> 1. Know the qualities needed for the credit controller
> 2. Understand how to provide in house training for all personnel who will have an effect on the efficiency of the credit controller in regard to the collection of debts

The Selection Process

What Makes An Effective Credit Controller?

The office dragon or the office bully will not make a good credit controller: contrary to popular opinion. Clients do not take kindly to being verbally bullied by people trying to extract money from them. Instead a more honey tongued method is needed. There is nothing wrong with using a little charm to persuade clients to part with their money. In terms of the client care relationship it works wonders. Whilst it is excessive to say that the idea of the collector is to have the client think that it was pleasure to pay his bill, it should certainly not leave him feeling disgruntled.

Necessary Character Traits – Quick Of Wit And Slow Of Temper

The credit controller should be able to hold their own in conversation, *i.e.* not let the client lead the conversation away from the objective of the call (which was to get a payment promise). Tenacity is therefore essential. The controller should be tactful yet firm, persuasive whilst understanding and above all be able to keep calm under extreme pressure, be it either pressure of work or verbal pressure from the client.

The ability to develop good administration skills and to be organised are a must. The credit controller must be someone who is able to plan ahead yet think on their feet when necessary.

The credit controller must be numerate, *i.e.* able to do basic mathematics with regards to amounts owing. Training should always be given with regard to a practice's accounts package, and the credit controller needs to be able to master a system within a short period of time. Failure to do so will make it impossible for a fully functional cash collection system to be implemented.

Candidates from agencies will probably have a score sheet showing their abilities with regards to accounts experience *i.e.* book keeping skills, purchase ledger experience, credit control experience. It is a worthwhile exercise to set up an in house score sheet, which can be given to candidates for credit control positions, for example the one opposite.

ACTIVITY	4 Good	3 Working Knowledge	2 Basic Experience	1 No Experience
Credit Control				
Cashiering				
Purchase Ledger				
COMMENTS				

S2 – Score Sheet

Having the relevant skills is all well and good but most importantly the credit controller must be able to see him or herself as part of a wider team than just credit control, and, like fee-earners, they should appreciate that they depend on the clients for their work.

Practical Training – For The Credit Controller

Law firms are different to other commercial ventures. One of the most commonplace sources of confusion for a credit controller new to the legal work place is a lack of understanding of legal terminology. For example, a credit controller may ring up a fee earner regarding an outstanding account, only to be told that the bill will not be paid until the assets are realised, or that the funds are dependent on a Garnishee Order. A list of basic legal terminology with relation to debt recovery is always useful. Also useful would be a general grounding of the legal departments and what they do within the practice. This introduction to the legal environment should be simple and informative. For example, in the conveyancing department, explanations could be given as to the various disbursements which are incurred such as Land Registry Fees, what these are, who pays them and when they are paid out. Giving the credit controller this information enables them to not only to have a basic knowledge of the workings of the other departments but will enable them to be able to carry out their own function more efficiently. Various products are available to perform this function, from dictionaries to audio cassettes and CD-ROMs.

Training: Solicitors Accounts Rules

A key aspect of training must be to ensure that the controller fully understands the Solicitors Accounts Rules in so far as they will relate to credit control. A copy of the Rules should be given to the credit controller with explanatory notes. The sections which would directly apply to credit control are as follows:

1. Rule 4(b) relating to the payment on account of costs
2. Rule 5A which deals with the part and full payment of bills
3. Rules 7 (a) ii, iii and iv which relates to the drawing from client accounts 9 (2)
4. Rule 9 (2) (a) (b) and (c)(I) and (ii) which relates to the paying of funds into the office account.

> *Note:* Specific client instructions given by the client takes precedence over the Rules.

Fee earners are responsible for the conduct of their files, but credit control should be aware of the basic rules governing the movement of funds through the file. For example, if a bill is paid, which has included disbursements relating to Counsel's, agent's or expert's fees, which are unpaid at the time of receipt of funds, then the part of the monies which cover those disbursements must be paid into the client account. If disbursements have been paid out already, then the monies must be paid into the office account.

Sometimes payments can be split between client monies and monies for invoices. The money should be treated as though two separate parts, and the bill money paid to the office account, and the client monies to the client account. Alternatively all funds may be paid into the client account, but only if the transfers to office are done within 7 days (Rule 5A). This gives the fee earner ample time to sort out the payment of disbursements.

Credit controllers should note that funds should *never* be moved out of the client account without the express authority of the fee earner in charge of the file who will in turn have to have obtained the authority of the client

Training: The Accounts System Of The Practice

Although the credit controller (unless doubling up for a cashier in smaller practices) will rarely, if ever, post receipts to the system they should be given thorough training on the particular accounts package operated by the practice. This is usually best done by the cashier, who can and should help the credit controller with the system until such time as they are able to 'fly solo' with regard to allocating funds. If the credit controller is left without this training they will never be able to understand the movements on an account. This will have a two fold effect. Firstly, they will be unable to decipher how much the client owes, especially if it is a multiple matter account, with funds regularly being paid in and out. Secondly, as this will lead to the credit controller being unable to allocate payment received properly, the workload of the cashier(s) will increase as they will have to check and redo any wrong chits.

Training: Who Pays In The Receipts?

There are two answers to this. The fee earners or the credit controller. Both are acceptable in terms of practical application, but only if the system for paying in is strictly adhered to.

Fee Earner Paying In

Some practices have the procedure whereby all cheques are sent with the daily post down to the fee earners to look at, acknowledge and pay in. This system will be successful **only** if the fee earner does pay the cheque in straight away, *i.e.* before close of banking. A busy fee earner may develop the unfortunate habit of sitting the cheques on file and forgetting them. The problem which may and often does occur with this method is that, if credit control does not get to see the cheques arriving, then they may ring the client up for payment, when he has already paid. Obviously when the cheque is paid in it may not get posted immediately so to the credit controller the account still looks outstanding.

In most circumstance, this will not cause any major problem. The client will merely state when he sent the cheque, and the credit controller can follow it up internally (*i.e.* ask the fee earner if they have it). A potential fiasco which could occur is if the credit controller has been waiting for a cheque from the client in response to a Letter Before Action and goes onto issue proceedings thinking that the cheque has not arrived.

It is up to the credit controller to ascertain that the cheque has not arrived, but if the fee earner misplaced it, or is away and no one has dealt effectively with the post there will be obvious problems.

With regard to training the fee earners in this matter, emphasis should be made with regard to banking deadlines and the problems which may occur if they do not comply. If a fee earner is away, his post should be gone through by another fee earner, and they should take responsibility for paying in the cheque.

Credit Controller Paying in

This method ensures that the credit controller knows which bills have been paid on a daily basis. The important thing here is to keep the fee earner informed so that they may acknowledge receipt of the cheques to their clients should they wish to.

Chits for office receipts should be always clearly and correctly made out and copies should be sent to the fee earner to hold on file.

Individual practices will use paying in chits particular to them, but the basic information which should be include by the credit controller when filling one out is:

1 Client's Name and Number
2 Date
3 Amount of being paid
4 Method of Payment (BACS, Cheque, Credit Card or Cash)
5 Bills number to be allocated with payment
6 Who the Payer is.
7 Special Instructions (i.e. the fee earner may have requested that the cheque be specially cleared.

Training: Client To Office Transfers

The credit controller should know that client funds should only ever be transferred to the office account for payment of a bill, with the authority of the fee earner, who in turn will have received the authority of the client.

As with the paying in of external payments, transfer chits should be clearly and accurately recorded. In particular the name of the authoriser of the transfer should noted down, should it be needed for future reference.

Training: Collections

Which Debts To Chase?
A practice's ledger may have a few debts on it, or again, it may have hundreds on it. The best method for deciding which debts to put most effort into is to use the Pareto Principle. Essentially, this states that 20% of the debtors will hold 80% of the value of the entire ledger. Therefore by chasing that 20% the credit controller should have more chance on recouping greater value. But remember all debts should be chased at some point. Every little helps keep the profits up!

Instalment Arrangements: Sympathy Coupled With Business Sense
Clients may ask for payment facilities and it should be clearly stated in the Credit Management Policy who is to authorise staggered

payments. If the credit controller is allowed to arrange instalment payments, before discussing this with the client they should seek advice from the fee earner as to the financial circumstances of the client. (The client could just be delaying payment for the sake of it or again there could be a genuine cash flow problem.)

Certainly clients who ask for this facility should be treated sympathetically: it could be that the cash flow problem is merely temporary and when they come out of it, they will remember the practice as helpful. But remember that legal practices are by no way immune to cash flow problems and this should be considered when deciding on the value and time scale of the instalments. The longer the bill takes to be paid the more likely it is to become a bad debt.

Clients Who Pay Twice

If the client for some reason pays a bill twice, this should be refunded immediately.

If the client has paid a number of bills with one cheque and only one of the bills has been double paid, the funds should be paid into the client account and distributed out to the outstanding bills in the office account. A cheque should then be raised for the surplus funds and the client refunded.

A checklist for collectors is presented at the end of this chapter, highlighting problem avoidance procedures.

Inter Departmental Training

Relationship Between The Fee Earner And The Credit Controller

What needs to be emphasised is that both the fee earner and the credit controller are working for the same practice for the good of the practice. A little appreciation and understanding of what each other does will go a long way for the smooth running of a collections system.

Whilst it is obvious that fee earning and credit control are two entirely separate professional functions, they are both *professional*. Therefore it is essential that both parties extend courtesy toward each other, communicate with each other and co-operate.

Professional Courtesy

Everybody has the right to be treated courteously. It should never be the case that either the credit controller or the fee earner be unapproachable. It must be appreciated by each person that just because they are overworked does not mean that everybody else is sat around with very little or nothing to do. In a successful practice, credit controller has just as much to do as a secretary or fee earner.

The basic problem is that very rarely does a fee earner know the realities of proper credit control any more than a credit controller knows exactly the work which goes into each case. The unenlightened fee earner assumes that credit controller merely picks up the phone and demands money, usually unpleasantly. The uninformed credit controller for their part generally believes that the fee earner merely speaks into the dictation machine all day. This problem can easily be remedied by a brief but informative induction session, given internally to all concerned parties.

Communication

Crystal balls are not standard issue for either fee earner or credit controller. Verbal or written communication between the two parties is essential.

If the credit controller is advised by the client that there is a problem/query, they should let the fee earner know *immediately* either by phone, memo or e-mail. They should never take it upon themselves to either comment on the query or decide that the client is just using the excuse as a delaying tactic, and so ignore what is said and keep it to themselves.

Complaints of *any* nature should always be taken seriously and need to be handled as quickly and efficiently as possible. Damage limitation is the main objective, so it is imperative that all relevant parties are informed of the query/complaint immediately, with a period of time for sorting it agreed and kept to.

For his or her part, the credit controller may know that the client is in serious financial trouble and should let the fee earner know before they incur more costs. Take this scenario from Slap Dash & Co:

> Slap Dash & Co have a client owing £5000.00. The credit controller has had difficulty getting any kind of information from the client as to when they will pay. The client has levied a variety of excuses to delay payment, and the Purchase Ledger has now taken to not answering telephone calls. Whilst attempting to contact the client again, the credit controller chats to one of the client's receptionists who lets it slip that several staff have been laid off suddenly. The inference being that the company is in severe financial difficulties and may go down.
>
> Rather than pass this information on the to the relevant fee earner, the credit controller ignores it as unimportant idle gossip. The client has an expensive litigation case starting and obviously does not intimate to the fee earner that they are in trouble. The fee earner goes ahead with the case and incurs expenses relating to Counsel's and Expert Witness's Fees. The client goes into liquidation and the practice is left to bear the costs of the disbursements as well as having to write of all the profit costs.
>
> Had the credit controller relayed their information to the fee earner as soon as they had got it this could have been avoided.

Credit control may be able to pass background information such as that a particular client always queries invoices as a standard delaying tactic. By the same token if the fee earner is informed of a genuine problem by the client, they should let credit control know so that they can put a hold on chasing procedures. Nothing annoys a client more than being chased for funds when they have informed the fee earner or credit controller that they are waiting an answer to a query. Communication on both sides can eliminate the possibility of upsetting the client.

There is nothing to gain in terms of power politics by keeping 'secrets' from each other.

Cooperation

If a fee earner has a genuine reason why a bill should not be chased, he should inform credit control of that reason, in order that it can be logged and the necessary action taken to stop chasing.

"Because I say so" is not a good reason to stop chasing. Neither is

"Because the client is a personal friend and you'll offend him."

What can be said is:

"Mr Smith is a personal friend of mine, I'll contact him myself with regard to payment and let you know the outcome".

The credit controller can then note this in the log and the call the fee earner back to find out what is happening if the fee earner does not let them know. Both parties know where they stand and neither has had their toes stepped on.

If a fee earner receives new client addresses or telephone numbers they should let credit control know. If they are able to put additional "pressure" on the client to pay, they should do so.

Courtesy, Communication and *Co-operation* are the keys to the fast and efficient collection of debt which will greatly assist in producing a profitable healthy practice with harmonious personnel relations.

Outside Training

Outside training course on credit control can be off putting because of cost. However, the benefit of attending these courses should not be underestimated. No matter how experienced a credit controller is, there is always more to learn. By going on the courses the credit controller will have the benefit of being able to talk to colleagues about chasing methods and may be able to bring new methods into the practice which will be of benefit in terms of improved cash collection.

Also available for further training are the Institute of Credit Management Courses. These cover basic credit control skills through to more advanced skills levelled at those credit controllers who wish to further their careers and become Credit Managers. Information relating to the ICM courses can be got from *Credit Management* the Journal of the ICM and further information can be got from the ICM itself at:

The Institute of Credit Management
The Water Mill
Station Road
South Luffenham
Oakham
Leicestershire LE15 8NB

Achievements

1. The practice should now be equipped to select a credit controller
2. Training for the credit controller and other personnel with regard to the practicalities of debtor payments and co-operation, should now be within the reach of every size and type of firm.

Chapter 11

Tips For The Credit Controller For Basic Problem Avoidance

Credit controllers can help themselves by carrying out basic checks prior to initiation of collection methods. These will prevent angering and offending the client (and the fee earner) whilst giving the impression that the firm is unprofessional and sloppy. The credit controller needs to keep their wits about them.

System-based information should be used to its full advantage prior to chasing. Checks should be made with relation to databases, the accounts system and bills for the information needed. The checklist overleaf is a list of potential pitfalls which can be avoided if checks are carried out prior to chasing collections.

CHECKLIST FOR CREDIT COLLECTIONS

1. **Is the name and address of the client current and correct?**
   There is little point in sending a letter to someone who no longer lives at that address.

2. **Is the matter Private & Confidential?**
   Take care in checking this. Most matters are of a sensitive matter, in particular employment matters. If the bill is Private and Confidential care should be taken as to who the original was sent to. Note that sometimes there will have been a covering letter sent with the bill and that the bill may therefore not be marked Private and Confidential. If the credit controller suspects (by looking at the type of matter the bill covered) that it may be for a certain person's eyes only, then a call should be put through *to the fee earner* for clarification and a name.

3. **Ensure the bill has been sent out**
   All bills should be sent out as a matter of course. However check the file to make sure that no memo has been sent stating the contrary.

4. **Ensure that there are no unresolved queries**
   Check on file to see if there are any notes relating to queries. If so, check that these have been resolved prior to chasing.

5. **Check the client account and ensure all transfers which should have been done, have been done**
   It may be that funds on account of costs have been paid to the client account in error and are awaiting transfer. Never move the monies without the fee earner's authority and alway write who gave the authority on the request chit. A copy should be sent to the fee earner for the file.

   Sometimes bills are sent to accounts receipted but the funds are not always brought across to pay the bill on the system. Again double check with the fee earner in question, and once approved, arrange for the transfers.

6   Check for BACS Payments
    Some clients will pay by BACS, both private clients (usually instalments) and more often the corporate sector. These should be checked everyday and allocated on a daily basis.

7   **Communicate**
    Speak to the fee earners if there is a problem, or if there is something strange about the account. For example, a bill may have been issued against the wrong client. By communicating with the fee earners, rather than going ahead, the credit controller shows themselves to be a thinking person rather than an automated "collections robot".

Conclusion To Part Two

The setting up of a *professional*, *proactive* and *positive* Credit Management System should be considered by all practices, regardless of size. The debtors ledger is the most important asset of any business and it should be treated accordingly.

This section has covered:

- the theory behind the setting up of a policy
- practical applications and the
- selection and training of personnel

all of which are vital to make up an efficient and effective Credit Management System.

Part III

Reporting

Chapter 12

Debtors Reporting

Introduction	138
Fee Earner Attitudes	139
What Format Should The Reports Take?	139
The Flow Of Information	140

Chapter 12

Debtors Reporting

Introduction

Trying to run a practice regardless of size without any financial information, particularly with regard to debtors levels, would be akin to driving a car without a steering wheel. Information, even if presented in the most simplistic format is an essential component of practice life: if the management wants to be able to plan and co-ordinate for the long term future of the practice whilst at the same time be able to react to current situations or crises which may present themselves.

This section is intended to be a practical guide through what is generally regarded as the most complex area of Credit Management within a practice – the formatting and understanding of a debtors reporting structure. Debtors reports are essential. They provide a medium by which the management of the practice can see immediately if the theory of its credit policies are working out in reality. Basically Debtors Reports are the highway by which the management can see whether the practice is converting its debtors into cash at an acceptable rate.

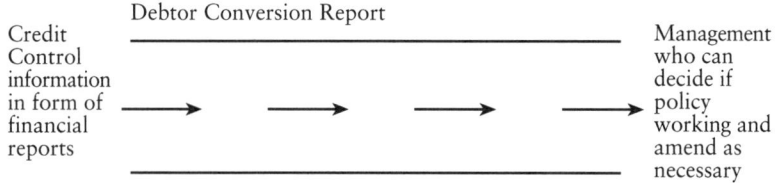

Figure 6: The Highway to Management Information

Fee Earner Attitudes

Some fee earners still regard any type of financial reports with trepidation and sometimes downright hostility. It is not uncommon for monthly reports to be consigned to the waste bin without being read; nor is it uncommon for those fee earners at some point later in the month to complain that they did not know that their client still had not paid his bills! This is unacceptable particularly in these days of fierce competition and tight finances. Financial information, particularly in the area of debtors, is important for ALL fee earners to read and understand. Accordingly this section explains the importance not only for practices to devise the debtor reports but also to understand them. Financial reports, particularly debtor reports, must no longer be the preserve of the accountant and auditors.

Good ideas are formed on a firm foundation of fact provided at regular intervals

The Managing Body (in whatever guise it takes, Managing Partner, Management Board or Sole Practitioner) needs know how the practice is performing at all times. To this end financial information needs to be produced on a regular basis. It is no use having reports once or twice a year. It is both difficult and financially unsound to have to sort problems several months down the track, and in the worst case the practice could be effectively lost before the problem is even noticed! Reports generated should enable the management to see any potential crises on a regular, almost immediate basis (at most one month old). They can then make the necessary contingency plans to alleviate or contain a problem. It goes without saying that the information has to be accurate. Making plans based on inaccurate information is not a viable option for any practice.

What Format Should The Reports Take?

The best kind of Financial Report is one which is simple to understand, concise and holds a short written commentary for those not figure orientated. Some practices issue reams and reams of financial data in the forms of graphs, charts and columns of figures which serve only to overload and confuse the average fee earner.

It should be remembered that firstly a fee earner's time is money, and secondly that he has chosen to specialise in law not accountancy. Time taken reading the monthly financial reports is non chargeable. Therefore the reports should be kept as pertinent to the fee earner and easy to follow as possible. In real terms the less immediately understandable a report the more chance it has of ending in the waste bin – unread! In short, the intention of any report should be to inform not confuse.

As financial reports should be the basis on which the practicalities of running of the practice are governed, it is essential that their formats should be set out to show certain criteria. They should show both the present position of the practice, with a comparative historical performance. They must also be consistent in their analyses, *i.e.* they should compare like for like. For example debtors at 60–90 days for May should have a comparison of the debtors aged 60–90 days the previous month and 60–90 days at the same period last year. Failing to keep comparisons consistent makes the financial data meaningless. It cannot be stressed enough that if good and practical policy decisions are to be made, accurate and useful information needs to be presented.

The Flow Of Information

The Managing Body should be able to use the financial information in a report to plan for the both the short and long term future of the practice using the resources available to them. The financial reporting structure is the highway for information to pass back and forwards in the practice. There should always be a constant flow of information and feedback on this highway between the people carrying out the day to day running of the practice and the Managing Body. This should result in maximum usage of resources coupled with firm control over the outgoings of the practice.

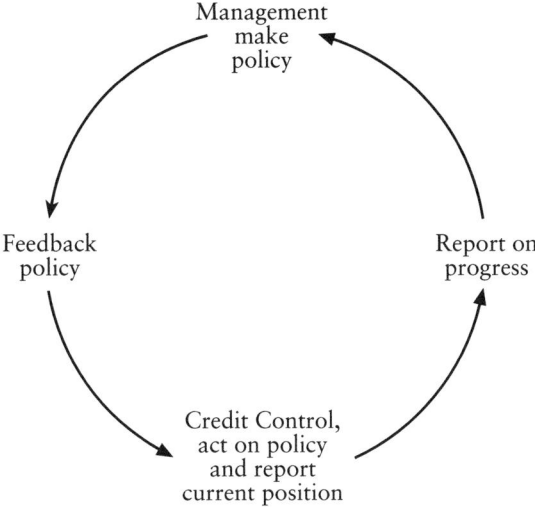

Figure 7: Flow of information

How The Information Flow Works

The Managing Body should work with the people doing the day to day legal work to improve *how* they are carrying out their duties based on the information that they are getting via the reports. Then the people carrying out the work should in their turn send information back, to inform the Managing Body whether their ideas are working or not.

The Particular Importance Of The Debtor Report

A full set of Financial Accounts of a practice will cover a number of key areas, such as WIP, unbilled Disbursements, Fees, Time Analysis, Profit & Loss and of course Debtors etc.. However, whilst for the majority of smaller and individually run practices a full range of data may not be required, it is essential for **ALL** practices, to know how much potential working capital is tied up in Debtors.

Put very basically:

Bills not paid = Cash not coming in = Cash flow problems.

There are the only two ways that the Managing Body is going to know about the above situation. Either regular and accurate debtor reports or the Bank Manager ringing up! Everyone knows which is preferable.

> By the end of Part III you should be able to:
>
> 1   Understand both the need and usefulness of debtor reports
> 2   Design a series of reports suitable for the individual needs and resources of your practice.

Chapter 13

Preparation For A Reporting Structure

The Importance Of The Database	144
Starting Off	144
How To Pass The Information From Fee Earner To Database Inputter	145
Upkeep Of The Database	150

Chapter 13

Preparation For A Reporting Structure

The Importance Of The Database

There is a favourite saying of credit managers that collections "begin at the beginning" *i.e.* that the lead up to the issue of the bill is of paramount importance to the bill being paid. Similarly financial reporting is dependent upon the right information being input in the first place. This chapter deals with the importance of having an accurate database system. It runs through some of the most common areas of error which have knock on effects, not only on the production of debtor reports but to the day to day running of the practice and most importantly, the way the practice is viewed by its clients.

> *Objectives*
>
> 1 Know the most common areas of error and be able to look out for them
> 2 Understand the importance of an accurate and up to date database.

Starting Off

Most practices now have some sort of computer system on which client details will be entered. Who does the data inputting will depend on the size and structure of the practice. A Sole Practitioner might enter and maintain the data himself. A medium sized practice may have a cashier entering client information. A larger practice may have a dedicated database operator, or a team of operators. However, regardless of who does the inputting, the information they will be inputting will come from those fee earners or members of the support staff who have had first contact with the client.

How To Pass The Information From Fee Earner To Database Inputter

Simple forms such as the example shown below can be used as a method of conveying new client information to the database operators. The amount of detail included on a database form will depend upon the sophistication of the computer system and the requirements of the practice. The most basic facility needed is simply to enter the client's name and address. Some databases will include marketing information, to track cross-selling opportunities *i.e.* whether clients should be informed about other legal services the practice may provide, or what are their sporting interest etc. (*Note*: if setting up a database for the first time, check that the practice is registered with the Data Protection Registrar.)

Some may have credit limits entered which will help monitor exposure levels by filtering onto exposure reports. It should be remembered though that the longer and more complex the forms are to fill out, the more unlikely it is that they will be completed by a busy fee earner, who simply wants to get on and put time on the file.

CLIENT DATA INFORMATION FORM

CLIENT NUMBER		MATTER NO	

SURNAME/ COMPANY NAME	
FORENAMES	
CONTACT NAME	

ADDRESS

BUILDING	
STREET	
TOWN	
COUNTY	
POSTCODE	

TEL NO (WORK)		TEL NO (HOME)	
FAX NO		MOBILE NO	
E MAIL		DX NO	

MATTER DESCRIPTION	

DEPARTMENT		WORK TYPE	
FEE EARNER		PARTNER RESPONSIBLE	
LEGAL AID?		CREDIT LIMIT	

DATE	

CL7 – Client Data Information Form

Essential Information

It should be the policy of the practice to make certain areas of information compulsory for fee earners to complete. These areas should include:

1   The Client's Full Name

2   The Client's Full Address

3   The Billing Address (if different)

4   The Client's Telephone Number
    (This will assist the Credit Controller who will be using the data information available to aid the collection of payments.)

5   A Fax Number (if available)

6   How the Client is Funded
    (This will make the difference as to whether the client is included in chasing procedures or not. If the client is funded by Legal Aid or Legal Expenses Insurance, for example, policy and procedures must be different and reporting should be separately identifiable from general debtors.)

7   The Contact Name
    (*i.e.* the person who authorised the work and with whom the fee earner is dealing. This will help credit control approach the right person for payment, whilst preventing the possibility of embarrassing the client, by going to a general purchase ledger for payment. This is particularly important if the matter is private and confidential, but the contact point is in the workplace.)

To make it easier for the fee earner to see at a glance which information they *must* enter, the appropriate boxes on the Client Data Information Form could be shaded. It may be feasible that the file not be opened for the fee earner until the information is included.

Accurate Information Only Please!

Whatever information is entered it is essential that it is accurate. Once entered onto the system the client will be given either an alpha numeric or purely numeric identifier, depending on the type of system used. This client code or account number forms the central reference point against which all individual transactions are carried out, *i.e.* the inputting of time sheets and disbursement recording. It will also appear on all bills. This code also will be the basis on which any reports relating to client management will be generated, including debtors reports, WIP balances and client balances etc..

What Happens If The Database Is Wrong?

Setting up a client wrongly, for example putting on the wrong address, will have a knock on effect to several areas of the practice, including credit control and reporting. Take this scenario at Slap Dash & Co:

> Mr Smith is allocated the number 1234.5. Through the automated database, his address is wrongly accepted as 23 Lock Green Drive, which is actually another Mr Smith's address. Francis the fee earner addresses his bill according to the system records. Mr Smith gets a bill which is not his. He will do one of two things. Ring up the practice and ask what they are doing, or ignore it and be chased by credit control unless the mistake is noticed before the expiry of the credit terms. Either way, his view of the expertise and professionalism of the practice can only be diminished, and there is a possibility that in future he will go elsewhere.
>
> Meanwhile the Mr Smith who should have been sent the bill has enjoyed extensive credit and the matter to which the bill relates is less immediate. The older the matter, the harder to chase – so the firm loses both ways.

To avoid this both the fee earner and database operator should ensure that what they have entered is correct. Verification can be done simply, by the sending to the fee earner a confirmation slip or label detailing what has been entered onto the database. The fee earner should then check it against the files he has set up for the client. It is better to rectify inaccurate information sooner rather than later and certainly before the client learns of the error.

User Error

Even if the database is accurately set up, mistakes will still happen and every effort should be made to avoid them. The simplest mistake to make is for fee earners and their secretaries to accidentally input wrong information onto time sheets or bills. Misreading or transposing a couple of figures are very easy and common mistakes to make, so care must be taken to guard against this. Cross checking what the database actually says is vital. Below is scenario of what can happen if a client number is transposed.

> Francis the Fee Earner does a bill for Instant Rich, on their purchase of Big Inc. The number for that file is 2345.6.5 however, when the bill is dictated, Frances accidentally says 2345.5.6 which is an entirely different matter. Instant Rich pay their bill but of course there is no bill to allocate it against on that file number. Nobody checks to see whether there is a bill for that much on Instant Rich's account as a whole, or asks Francis if he knows why the client has paid the money. The cheque is duly returned to the client. The client is left with the impression that the practice is incompetent.

Another problem which may ensue from not putting the correct client number on the bill is that the credit controller, particularly if there is an automatic system, may end up chasing the wrong person for payment. In fact, not only will the scenario affect the credit controller, but it will also affect financial reporting. The client who has wrongly had the bill allocated to him may exceed his exposure level. It will also be shown on the debtor reports as his bill. Accordingly a client may be refused legal services and the practice lose twice.

Great care must be exercised when first putting client details onto the database and a checking loop put in to ensure that they are verified by fee earners.

Upkeep Of The Database

It is very important that there is regular housekeeping of the database. Information about changes will usually come through the fee earner who will be in direct contact with his client. However, sometimes the credit controller may be informed of a change and he should inform both the fee earner and the database inputter of the details or make those changes if practice procedures allow. Problems which occur with outdated information are numerous, for example:

- A name change not done can cause offence: a client may have had a unpleasant divorce and reverted to her former name or remarried.
- If a client has died, his relatives will not be happy to receive letters addressed to the deceased.
- If an old address is on the system there will be problems with regards to billing and the collecting of bills. If there is an automated billing and/or credit system it will pick up the address on the database. Even if the bills are done manually, the chances are that the address used will be the one on the database, and the credit controller will follow the address on the bill.
- Another reason to keep up to date with addresses is that if the client has moved, bills which may have been issued will end up being written off, because the client is no longer at that address and he cannot be traced. (This is particularly relevant in domestic conveyancing and matrimonial work, where the client may leave the matrimonial home.)

Internal Housekeeping

It is not only client information which needs to be current: internal changes also need to be noted onto the database. For example, when a fee earner leaves, his files will be transferred into another fee earner who is taking over the conduct of those files. If this is not done, then when financial reporting is undertaken, fee earners who have left are still shown to be billing, have outstanding WIP, disbursements and outstanding debtors.

In addition if a file is passed to another fee earner to work on permanently, the file should be transferred to their name. They are then shown both as the person responsible for that file and the internal contact point. Information such as the above can be purveyed to the data inputter by simple amendment form such as the one below:

CLIENT DATA AMENDMENT FORM

| CLIENT NUMBER | | MATTER NO | |

| NAME CHANGE/ CONTACT CHANGE | |

ADDRESS

BUILDING	
STREET	
TOWN	
COUNTY	
POSTCODE	
TEL NO (WORK)		TEL NO (HOME)	
FAX NO		MOBILE NO	
E MAIL		DX NO	

| FEE EARNER CHANGE | | PARTNER RESPONSIBLE | |
| LEGAL AID STATUS CHANGE | | CREDIT LIMIT CHANGE | |

| DATE | |

CL8 – Client Data Amendment Form

The gathering of new or updated information by osmosis, on which some practices rely, is not the best way to ensure an accurate database. The database (whether held on paper or on computer) is going to be the basis for both the day to day running of the practice and management reports. Wrong client information can only have negative effects on practices. A well regulated and verified system for management of data is essential for all types of practice. Good, practical management is founded on accurate information at all levels.

Achievements

1 Controllers should now know the most common areas of error and be able to look out for them; and
2 Understand the importance of an accurate and up to date database.

Chapter 14

The Structure And Format Of Reports

Introduction	154
How Often Should The Debtors Reports Be Produced?	154
Who Should Produce The Report?	155
To Whom And What To Include?	155
How Should Debtors Information Be Presented?	159
Feedback	160
The Debtors Report As An Aid To Cash Flow Projection	160
Caveats	161
Summing Up The Debtor Report	162

Chapter 14

The Structure And Format Of Reports

Introduction

The Debtors Report is one of the most useful tools a practice can have to see how it is doing in terms of financial success. It can be produced in either a simplistic or complex format, depending upon the requirements of an individual practice. For practices which do not already have an established reporting structure, the thought of initiating one may seem daunting. The aim of this chapter is to show how simple it is to set up such a system and to examine the benefits which will ensue.

> ### Objectives
> 1. Set up a basic debtor reporting structure
> 2. Understand the usefulness of the debtor reports in relation to the effective management of the practice

How Often Should The Debtors Reports Be Produced?

Any financial report should be provided on a regular basis. Ad hoc reporting serves little purpose as patterns and trends cannot be monitored. Debtor Reports should be produced once a month. Exactly when in the month depends upon the individual practice's cut off for month end. Certainly reports should be done no later than the second week of the following month or the information in the report will be hopelessly different from the current situation. The faster the reports can be produced and sent out, the faster they can be acted upon. It is particularly important in the case of debtors to get the information out and followed up by credit control as close to the month end as possible, to aid the chasing process. Most clients (particularly corporate) will pay at the month end. The credit controller will therefore need to be contacting clients in the first three weeks of the month to stand any chance of being included on end of month payment runs.

Who Should Produce The Report?

The most likely candidate to produce the report will obviously depend on the size, structure and resources of the practice. A sole practitioner should be able to procure a simplistic debtors reports, as he will have a list of the bills he has done. This could quite easily be on paper. For a medium to large practice a practice manager or member of the accounts department, *e.g.* accountant or credit controller should be able to provide the debtors reports.

To Whom And What To Include?

A Fee Earners
   In some practices only partners receive financial information but it is to the advantage of the practice if all fee earners are sent copies of the debtors reports specific to them. They are closer to their particular matters than their senior. There is no reason to keep debtor levels a secret or to allow them to become the preserve of the credit controller and the partners. Nor should it be expected that fee earners know automatically what is outstanding and what is not. By providing them with reports on a regular basis, they are able to see which of their clients have failed to pay and take an informed view as to whether they should continue working for them. If a fee earner is not told his client is a bad risk how is he to know?

B Departmental Heads
   Further up the practice structure some practices will be split into departments headed by a particular partner. The Department Head should be sent the information relevant to their department, *i.e.* how the fee earners in their department are doing on an individual basis and how their department is doing in comparison to the rest of the firm, or against the firm's plan.

C Managing Body
   Obviously the management of the practice should receive the most detailed reports concerning all fee earner activity in all departments as they will need to see an overall picture on how everyone and every department in the practice is performing.

What to Include?

The actual look and complexity of the information for the debtors report will of course depend on the needs of the individual practice. For example a sole practioner could input his bill details onto an Excel spreadsheet and sort according to date order, marking bills off as they get paid. Larger firms will be able to run off an aged debt from their accounts system.

The structure of the debtors reports

The aged debtor reports should split bills into debtor periods for example 0–30 days, 31–60, 61–90, 91–180 etc. The date periods will depend upon the needs of each individual practice and should match their credit terms. The aged debt report can be sorted by date period, *i.e.* all the bills of the practice over in the 0–30 period, followed by all the bills raised that have reached the 31–60 period etc. Or it can be sorted by department and sub divided by fee earner.

The report should sub total each section and end with an overall practice total. This will aid the credit controller and accountant to begin to analyse the debtors progress as shown in chapter 14.

Examples of possible arrangements for the debtors report can be seen below:

Example 1	Example 2
Debtors by Date Period	Debtors By Department & Fee Earner
0–30 days list of bills sub total for bills 0–30 days 31–60 days list of bills sub total for bills 31–60 days etc **Total Debtors for Practice Overall**	Corporate Fee Earner 1 list of bills Sub total Fee Earner 2 list of bills sub total Sub total for Corporate Department Litigation Fee earner 1 list of bills Sub total for Litigation Department etc **Total Debtors for Practice Overall**

Within the list of bills certain information basic information should be included if the reports are to be of real use:

1 Client's Name & Number
 This will obviously act as an identifier
2 Matter Description
 This is a useful as the client may have several matters and bills raised at different dates and the credit controller can specify a particular bill on a specific matter.
3 Fee earner
4 Bill Date
 This acts as indicator of age.
5 Bill Number
6 Current amount outstanding
 (As opposed to the original amount of the Bill.) This is particularly necessary when bills are being paid by instalments.

Additional Information

Additional information could include showing the split of an individual bill into fees, disbursements and VAT. Also the original figure could be shown next to the current amount outstanding figure.

Further additions could be the partner in charge of the fee earner and partner in charge of the client.

Below are two suggested formats for the debtors report.

Cl No	Client Name	Matter	Fee Earner	Bill Date	Bill No	Amount Outstanding
123.2.1	Mr J Smith	Sale of 23 Hill Crest	JJ	25.4.98	125	253.36

Figure 8: Simple Debtors Report.

Or a more complex alternative

Client No	Client Name	Matter	Partner	Fee	Bill Date	Bill No	Bill Total	Profit Costs (£)	Disb (£)	VAT (£)	Amount o/s (£)
1232	Jones	MBO	KHE	JJH	12.5.98	1254	21737.50	18500.00	0.00	3237.50	5000.00

Figure 9: Complex Debtors Report.

How Should Debtors Information Be Presented?

The information might be presented in the form of a Credit Management Report or Debtors Report. The name of the report is up to the individual practice. What is important is that the report shows the financial information in a clear and consistent fashion, and that the format chosen is kept for the full financial year to aid comparative analysis.

A Debtors/Credit Management Report, if properly presented and understood can be much more than merely a list of all unpaid bills. It can pinpoint a variety of problems, which if left unattended may cause difficulties with regard to the cash flow of the practice. The report should be set up so that it shows a series of data tiers: beginning with the individual fee earner, moving up through the various divisions and finally ending with an overall view of the practice. It should in effect be like peeling an onion. Layer upon layer of information being peeled back until getting back to the central core which is of course the fee earner level.

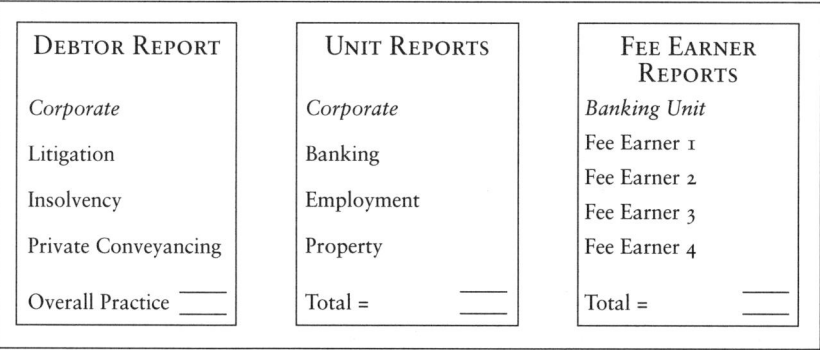

Figure 10: A layered report

The number of layers depends upon the size, set up and needs of each practice. Shown below is a guideline for the data tiers of information dependent upon practice size and structure. The more sub divisions a practice has, the more tiers of information it will need.

Large/Middle Multi Unit*	Small Multi Unit	Small Single Unit
Overall Practice Departmental Division Fee Earner	Overall Practice Departmental Fee Earner	Overall Practice Fee Earner

*Unit = type of law practices *e.g.* Corporate, Litigation, Family etc.

Feedback

Once the reports have been distributed, it is good idea for the credit controller to follow up with a visit or telephone call (depending on proximity) to each fee earner to discuss the debtors. This flow of information between fee earner and credit controller was highlighted in the previous section, under communication and co-operation. Both parties need to be aware of what is happening with debtors and the monthly debtor report is a good basis on which this movement of information can be based. For example with regard to older bills, the fee earner may be able to help with the collection process, or have information regarding other sources of payment such as a completion, from which the outstanding accounts will be paid. In respect of the new bills, the credit controller can check that they have been sent out on time, and that they were agreed with the client prior to their issue.

The Debtors Report As An Aid To Cash Flow Projection

The Debtors Report as well as enabling the examination of debtor levels, can also aid cash flow projection. This can be done by the provision by the report writer of an analysis of the debtors into sub divided into various categories. For example:

- those debtors who will pay;
- those who pay in instalments;
- those bills that will never be paid; and
- those who are in a temporary query situation.

A simple table, such as the one below, can give an indication of probable cash collection for the month ahead. The figures used would come from the credit controller who would obtain the information from clients and telephone logs, passing the information on to the report writer if not themselves.

£'s

Hold	Instalments	Taxation	Sued	Chasing	Total
10,000	26,500	3,000	11,000	170,000	220,500

Figure 11: Cash Collection Report

So of the £220,500 on debtors ledger, there is a possibility of obtaining £170,000 and whatever payment is due from the instalments.

Caveats

There are certain points to be taken into consideration before embarking on a programme of reporting. Firstly, it should be made clear that having the reports is not going to be a substitute for managerial decisions. They are merely going to aid the management in their policy creation.

Secondly, financial reports by their very nature can be easily misinterpreted or misunderstood, so it is advisable that the reports are accompanied by narratives, laying the findings of the reports out in as clear a manner as possible.

The report writer should also take account of anomalies, such as year end "billing binges" (yes, everybody does it!). Or certain cases which may provide either unusually high fees, or bills which will take a longer than average to settle, for example bills relating to insolvency cases. These examples will have a tendency to "throw" figures out in relation to averages or Aged Debtors percentage levels and should be noted in the commentaries.

Finally, it should be remembered that the report is based on the information at hand, on either a manual or the computer system. So ensure that prior to month end all transfers are done, all receipts are posted and any credit notes or write offs which should have been done have been done. Inaccurate reports lead to inappropriate management decisions.

Summing Up The Debtors Report

A good and constructive Debtors Report should be designed to be more than a basic listing of unpaid bills. The point of the Debtors Report is that it informs and enables the analysis of the debtor profile. This in turn will enable the management to see whether the Credit Policy is working and if any adjustments relating to credit control or fee earning staff need to be made. It will also alert the management to a possibility of a cash flow crisis, or whether the collection rates are going so well that they have working capital to reinvest, for example buy more computer equipment, employ more staff or (even) pay distributions to the partners. In other words it will provide the information to make policy decisions which will be of benefit to the practice.

Achievements

1. The controller and others should now be able to set up a basic debtors reporting structure; and
2. Understand the usefulness of the Debtors Reports in relation to the effective management of the practice

Chapter 15

Taking A Closer Look At A Debtors Report

The Aged Debt 164
A Simple Debtor Report – Debtor Days Analysis 165

Chapter 15

Taking A Closer Look At A Debtors Report

Debtors Reports can take on various formats, from a basic Aged Debt Printout to a Credit Management Report which provides debtors movement analyses by figures and graphs. Which format is most suitable to an individual practice will be dependent partly upon its needs and partly on its resources. The following chapters are intended to provide the reader with a step by step guide to a variety of reporting formats which may be of use. Examples of graphs are also given. Graphs can be of use, if coupled with commentaries and financial data, as they show trends very clearly. Graphs on their own, however, can be confusing and open to interpretation. The reports cited are by no means definitive and individual practices should create their own formats according to their structural needs. A general guide to the interpretation of the formats presented is also included with the aim of demystifying financial data.

> *Objectives*
>
> 1. To produce a simple debtor analyses measuring practice performance
> 2. To know what to look out for in the report

The Aged Debt

The Aged Debt report/print out, which is system generated on an automated system, is the base on which Debtor Reports are formed. However, it should be remembered that whilst the Aged Debtors will be an accurate representation of the debtor position, in effect it tells the practice very little. It is purely a listing of the debts owed at the current time. Rather like a recipe, it provides the ingredients for a feast, but in itself is unremarkable and indigestible. If the practice is to know whether the trends for increased debtors is up or down or cash flow is up or down, or whether particular fee earners have problems, then the raw ingredients have to be turned into a consumable product.

A Simple Debtor Report – Debtor Days Analysis

The simplest report based on the Aged Debt, which any practice regardless of size or account systems can produce is a listing of Debtor Days. This is a list of how long it is taking to convert bills to cash. The equation for this is very simple:

$$\frac{\text{Fees Outstanding}}{\text{Cumulative Fees Rendered}} \times 365 = \text{No of days outstanding.}$$

The figures can be done on a fee earner level, a department level or an overall level, depending with what the practice management feels comfortable. But even this most simplistic of reports, if taken at more than face value can reveal potential or established problems which otherwise could remain hidden.

Below is an example of a Debtor Days analysis report for Slap Dash & Co. The aim of the practice was to get the debtor days down to 60 days. Looking at the report it has done that. However, Slap Dash & Co do have a problem on their hands. But what is it?

SLAP DASH & CO
DEBTOR DAYS ANALYSIS AS AT 28 FEBRUARY 1998

Department	This month Debtor Days	Last Month Debtor Days	Variance +/-
Corporate Property	55	58	(3)
Corporate	40	45	(5)
Employment	130	142	(12)
Private Residential	18	18	-
General Litigation	55	56	(1)
Debtor Days for Practice	60	64	(4)

Figure 12: Debtor Days 1

Dissecting The Report

Supposing this was the first time a fee earner had seen this report. What is likely to be saying to him/her?

The first thing the fee earner should do is look at the title which states what the report is about. The table is a *Debtor Day Analysis*. This is a report informing the reader of how many days it is taking clients to pay their bills. In other words, it is a method for measuring cash conversion. Further it is a *Departmental Analysis* that is, it is looking at the practice as whole, but subdividing it into its specialist divisions.

The table gives three sets of figures, one current *This month*, one historical *Last month*, and a *Variance* figure which enables the fee earner to see at a glance whether the debtor days are increasing or decreasing. (It is a good idea, with historical data, to put variance figures in. It is exceptionally irritating, especially for busy fee earners who have limited time to have to work out by how much each figure is up or down. Reports should 'spoon-feed' information.)

The report can be read at two levels. The superficial level which reports on the overall practice status (the top layer of the onion) or on a more in-depth level which will reveal an interesting financial fact.

What This Report Says On The Overall Practice Level

Self evidently, the report tells the fee earner that the practice is improving its overall debtor days. Last month it had 64, this month it had 60: a decrease of 4. This would suggest that the credit controller and the practice policy as regards billing and overall credit management is working. With that in mind it would be quite feasible for the uniformed fee earner to put down the report and forget it until next month. The wise (or trained) fee earner will look at the report at lot more closely than that and cast his eye over the performance levels of the individual departments.

Looking At The Report At The Departmental Level

The report reveals an interesting and potentially worrying feature with regard to the individual departmental performances. One department has a much slower collection rate than the others. In fact it is the excellent collection rate of the other departments which is carrying it and making the overall debtor day figure for the practice seem in line with practice's anticipated target. On the surface this may not seem such a problem as long at the practice is doing alright overall, but no practice can really afford one department to drag down the general progress or in other words, not pull its financial weight. (Unless of course it is being used as a loss leader!) Remember that that department is still using up working capital in terms of wages, light, heating, equipment etc, regardless of whether or not its fees are being converted into cash. If further convincing is necessary, work out how much interest is being lost on a daily basis because of late payments!

What Could Be Going Wrong?
The reader needs to identify clearly and accurately the root of the problem, and to do this he needs to look at the next layer of debtor information – the fee earner level. This should reveal whether the problem is department wide or down to a few or even just one renegade fee earner who has chosen not to follow the Credit Management Policy.

There are several possible causes for late payments. One may be genuine: for example a large corporate client may have negotiated longer credit terms in exchange for volume business. However, more problematically, it may be that the fee earner (or Department in general) are not pre-agreeing bills with clients, billing at the wrong times, or even have offered their clients credit terms outside of the normal credit terms of the practice. All of these will have an effect on the conversion of debtors to cash, and need to be corrected as soon as possible, as the situation will only get worse if left to fester. If left, maybe other fee earners from other departments will follow suit, or clients given concessions in one department or by one fee earner will expect the same firm-wide. The problem can soon multiply across the practice. The result will of course cause chaos with the cash flow at some point in time.

No practice can afford to ignore potential problems like the above. The longer problems go unsolved the harder they are to rectify. Rather like a bill in some ways: the longer it takes to get paid, the less chance it has of being paid.

Sometimes reports bring bad news. If for example, debtor days are showing an increase, it is even more important to be able to discover the cause as quickly as possible. Using the same table as earlier the figures in Figure XX below have been rearranged to show a decrease in the efficiency of cash conversion.

SLAP DASH & CO
DEBTOR DAYS ANALYSIS AS AT 28 FEBRUARY 1998

Department	This month Debtor Days	Last Month Debtor Days	Variance +/-
Corporate Property	58	55	3
Corporate	45	40	5
Employment	142	130	12
Private Residential	18	18	-
General Litigation	56	55	1
Debtor Days for Practice	64	60	4

Figure 13: Debtor Days II

The practice will need to find out why this is the case as soon as possible in order to put it right before lasting damage is done. Possible reasons for upward trends can be varied. For example it could suggest that:

- the credit controller is not being as efficient as the practice would like;
- there may be a problem with the way the bills are being issued;
- maybe bills were not agreed, or
- there could be a problem with double billing (raising the same fee note twice),
- it may be that there is a specific large matter which has thrown the figures out.

All of the possible reasons need to be examined and eliminated until the real root cause of the problem is found, which of course will mean dissecting all level of information right down to the fee earner level.

Achievements

1 The production of a simple debtor report, and
2 The ability to understand the information presented in the report.

Chapter 16

Reports Within the Debtors Report

What The Credit Management/Debtors Report
Should Provide   172
The Complete Report   173
Summing Up The Usefulness Of Reports   182

Chapter 16

Reports Within the Debtors Report

The debtor day analyses report is the simplest of the debtors reports to produce. Without the aid of spreadsheets or graphs, it can reveal to the reader the financial state and the potential state of the practice, pinpointing accurately the root cause of any problems.

However, a full Credit Management/Debtors Reports is made up of a variety of debtor analyses which will form the basis from which the Managing Body will make decisions relating to Credit Policy. The following chapter is designed to show a number of debtor analyses which can be used to make up a Credit Management Debtors Report. The formats shown are both simple to produce and user friendly. The formats include both charts and graphs showing the progression of debtor conversion for the practice. The formats are suitable for all practices. The number of levels of information to be provided will depend upon the size and structure of each practice. Once the formats have been set up on a spreadsheet all that needs to be done is to update the figures and re-write the commentaries each month.

Objectives

1. To be able to assess the value of reports for your practice
2. To be able to produce a Credit Management Report

What The Credit Management/Debtors Report Should Provide

The aim of the Report is to give a full and accurate picture regarding the historical, current and future cash flow of the practice. The Report should show clearly trends or patterns in the debtors which will enable the Managing Body to assess the effectiveness of their Credit Policies.

Where Will The Information Come From?

The source of the information will come from the Aged Debt Report which will be generated from accounts system and the credit controller, who will be able to provide information on debtor status and daily cash collection.

Note: the following formats are by no way definitive. Each practice may have use for just some or all of the reports included and must decide on the most suitable format for itself.

The Complete Report

A good report should be set out in a logical and flowing sequence.

---

1   Introduction
2   Debtors Analyses (Various)
    a   Aged Debtor Level Analyses
    b   Debtor Days Analyses
    c   Debtor Status Analyses
    d   Daily Cash Collection Rates
3   Conclusion
4   Recommendations

---

1 **The Introduction**
   The report should start with an introduction, stating what the report is about, what it contains and why it has been written. Wording for the introduction will obviously be up to the report writer, but an example of what could be stated is shown below:

> **A Sample Introduction**
> The following report is an analysis of the debtor levels and cash collection activity of the practice using both historical and current data in the form of tables and graphs.
>   The report is split into three sections:
>
>   1. The Debtor Analyses,
>   2. Conclusions; and
>   3. Recommendations.
>
> The purpose of the report is to highlight trends which are apparent within debtors and to bring to the fore any problems which need particular attention.
>   The aim of the analysis is to enable the practice to evolve a more streamlined and effective approach to debt management and improve cash collection.

2 **The Debtor Analyses**
   After the Introduction has set the scene, the report should then show the various Debtors Analyses, each of which should be accompanied by a written commentary clearly stating what the figures as showing *i.e.* the trends and movements apparent from the figures. Graphs are optional. Some fee earners will find graphs an easy method of seeing trends, others may find them confusing. Whether they are included or not is dependent on whether users respond to them. Like the rest of the reports, once set up they are easy to update each month.

SLAP DASH & CO

Aged Debtors as at 30 JUNE 1998

Days	% of Debtors Totals	Grand Total	UNIT 1	UNIT 2	UNIT 3	UNIT 4
365+	4	3,254		3,254		
180–365	11	10,364		9,626	590	148
90–180	6	5,667	123	2,951	1,652	940
60–90	7	6,213		3,927	1,638	648
30–60	20	18,760	1,000	5,008	6,443	6,309
*0–30	52	48,541	2,077	16,951	15,834	13,678
	100	92,799	3,200	41,717	26,158	21,723

Aged Debtors as at 31 MAY 1998

Days	% of Debtors Totals	Grand Total	UNIT 1	UNIT 2	UNIT 3	UNIT 4
365+	8	6,697		6,697		
180–365	11	9,509		8,136	690	682
90–180	9	7,539	123	5,089	2,328	
60–90	5	4,205		1,762	1,504	940
30–60	17	14,010	228	8,015	4,203	1,564
*0–30	50	41,311	1,878	6,733	19,668	13,033
	100	83,272	2,228	36,433	28,392	16,219

Aged Debtors as at 30 April 1998

Days	% of Debtors Totals	Grand Total	UNIT 1	UNIT 2	UNIT 3	UNIT 4
365+	7	8,965	–	6,620		
180–365	14	19,612	–	6,435	790	682
90–180	16	21,222		8,301	2,383	–
60–90	18	24,532	–	1,575	473	88
30–60	6	7,947	–	2,806	2,638	2,503
*0–30	39	53,516	1,937	15,085	21,459	15,035
	100	135,794	1,937	40,823	27,743	18,308

Figure 14: Aged Debt Report: historic and current

This type of Debtor Analysis and graph details the overall aged debt level of the practice and the total of debtors for each department for the last three months. Thereby, the analysis is showing movement over a quarterly period. By having both the current month and the previous two the reader is able to see any trends which may be becoming established. The reader should be on the look out for departments which are increasing their number of older debtors or departments which have falling current debtors.

Note: A fall in the number of current debtors *i.e.* those aged 0–30 days, may not necessarily mean an increase in the level of payments in that period, it could mean that there are fewer bills being raised, and this is a trend which should be investigated. The graphs shown plot the course over the year, and give the reader a clear indication of the trends of debtors over the year. A line going upwards should only be seen for 0–30 days. All other lines should show a downward trend.

2b Debtor Days Analysis

SLAP DASH & CO

QUARTERLY DEBTOR DAYS ANALYSIS AS AT JUNE 1998

	Month 2		Month 1		Current Month	
Debt	April	Mar/Apr Variance +/-	May	Apr/May Variance +/-	June	Variance
Unit 1	59	5	55	- 4	52	- 3
Unit 2	46	1	40 -	- 6	42	+2
Unit 3	140	3	130 -	-10	135	+5
Unit 4	18	-	18	-	18	-
Average days	65	9	60 -	- 5	263	+1

Figure 15: Debtor Days Analysis

This analysis shows the progression of cash conversion for the practice over the last three months. The formula for this was shown on page 60. A variance table is shown in between the months to clearly show progress or otherwise.

2c Debtor Status Analysis

Status of Debts as at February 1998							
Debt	Hold	Instalments	Taxation	Sued	Chasing	Totals	Chasable %
Unit 1	617			208	11,434	12,259	93
Unit 2	13,738	371		2,374	116,142	132,625	88
Unit 3	4,836		420	1,147	124,434	130,837	95
Unit 4	24,629	8,262		45,768	168,638	247,297	68
£ TOTAL VALUE	43,820	8,633	420	49,497	420,648	523,018	

Figure 16: Debtor Status Analysis

The debtors have been split into a number of categories which themselves are divided into those immediately collectable and those not. The sorts of categories which are to be included are up to the individual practice, but a suggested categorisation is as follows:

1. **Instalments:**
   Bills which are paid on a weekly or monthly basis
2. **Suing**
   Bills which are the subject of legal proceedings as the normal channels of credit control have failed.
3. **Contingent Bills**
   Bills where payment is guaranteed but not until a certain event takes place. This could be a sale, completion or the end of a litigation case.
4. **Hold**
   Where the fee earner has put a stop on the normal chasing procedures. For example, the bills may be in query.
5. **Chasing**
   Bills that credit control are able to directly chase in accordance to the procedures laid down in the credit policy.

   Note: It is advised that a short commentary setting out what each category means, also accompanies this report.

This analysis is a particularly effective management tool as it clearly shows the overall value of debtors genuinely collectable and those debts which may not be collectable either in the short or long term. This will help with the monthly cash flow projections. The analysis can then be sub-divided into departments and fee earners. This will then show whether certain departments/fee earners make too much use of instalments, or certain departments try and get around the normal collection procedures by putting their bills on hold.

A particularly useful analysis to accompany this is a variance section. This can be done with a *This Month* v *Last Month* comparative as shown. The analysis can be set out to show either percentage of value or absolute monetary value for each unit/fee earner.

The table below shows the percentage of bills for each unit that are currently not available for Credit Control to collect *directly* from the client.

Variance	% Non Chaseable THIS MONTH	%Non Chaseable LAST MONTH	+/-
UNIT 1	45	67	(22)
UNIT 2	12	26	(14)
UNIT 3	46	31	15
UNIT 4	46	27	19

Figure 17: Debtor Status: Chasing

In this way the reader is easily able to assess whether the number of bills not available for chasing is going up, or if there is an increase in the number of bills put into suing, or if the use of instalments is increasing.

2d. Daily Cash Collection Analysis

Daily Cash Report for June 1998

Leeds	Manchester	Liverpool	London	Newcastle	Total Receipts	Date	Weekly Totals	Daily Average	Working Days
						01-Jun-98		–	1
						02-Jun-98		–	2
						03-Jun-98	–	–	3
						04-Jun-98		–	4
						05-Jun-98		–	5
						08-Jun-98		–	6
						09-Jun-98		–	7
						10-Jun-98	–	–	8
						11-Jun-98		–	9
						12-Jun-98		–	10
						15-Jun-98		–	11
						16-Jun-98		–	12
						17-Jun-98	–	–	13
						18-Jun-98		–	14
						19-Jun-98		–	15
						22-Jun-98		–	16
						23-Jun-98		–	17
						24-Jun-98	–	–	18
						25-Jun-98		–	19
						26-Jun-98		–	20
						29-Jun-98	–	–	21
						30-Jun-98		–	22
–	–	–	–	–	–		–		

Daily Cash Report for May 1998

Leeds	Manchester	Liverpool	London	Newcastle	Total Receipts	Date	Weekly Totals	Daily Average	Working Days
						01-May-98	–	–	1
						05-May-98		–	2
						03-Jun-98	–	–	3
						04-Jun-98		–	4
						05-Jun-98		–	5
						11-May-98		–	6
						12-May-98		–	7
						13-May-98	–	–	8
						14-May-98		–	9
						15-May-98		–	10
						18-May-98		–	11
						19-May-98		–	12
						20-May-98	–	–	13
						21-May-98		–	14
						22-May-98		–	15
						26-May-98		–	16
						27-May-98		–	17
						28-May-98	–	–	18
						29-May-98		–	19
–	–	–	–	–	–		–		

Daily Cash Report for April 1998

Leeds	Manchester	Liverpool	London	Newcastle	Total Receipts	Date	Weekly Totals	Daily Average	Working Days
					–	01-Apr-98	–	–	1
					–	02-Apr-98	–	–	2
					–	03-Apr-98		–	3
					–	06-Apr-98		–	4
					–	07-Apr-98	–	–	5
					–	08-Apr-98		–	6
					–	09-Apr-98		–	7
					–	14-Apr-98		–	8
					–	15-Apr-98	–	–	9
					–	16-Apr-98		–	10
					–	17-Apr-98		–	11
					–	20-Apr-98		–	12
					–	21-Apr-98	–	–	13
					–	22-Apr-98		–	14
					–	23-Apr-98		–	15
					–	24-Apr-98		–	16
					–	27-Apr-98		–	17
					–	28-Apr-98	–	–	18
					–	29-Apr-98		–	19
					–	30-Apr-98		–	20
–	–	–	–	–	–		–		

Figure 18: Daily Cash Collection Report

This analysis shows how much money is being received on a daily basis by the practice. Again the last three months' analyses are shown together to indicate whether the average daily cash collections are improving or not. If the practice has several branches, the analysis can be divided to show how each of the branches are performing. It should be stated whether the amount collected shows all the elements of the bill (*i.e.* profit costs, disbursements and VAT) or makes an allowance for disbursements and VAT. This can, of course, have an effect on profitability: for example, some bills will be "disbursement heavy".

The graph provided shows the daily cash collection pattern. This pattern should enable a projection of cash collection for the following month. So that if a monetary value of x is billed and is on the Aged Debt the practice should be able to expect x in for the following month. The graph should also allow the practice to be able to pinpoint high and low points in monthly cash collection, which can then be built into cash flow projections and budgets.

3 THE CONCLUSION TO THE REPORT

The aim of the conclusion is to emphasis to the reader the movement and trends shown in the analysis and on the graphs. The conclusion should be a factual critique of the debtors: it serves no purpose if it merely highlights the good points and tries to sweep the bad under the carpet.

A Sample Conclusion

The debt collection performance is continuing to show a steady improvement with cash collections up to x. However, there is an increase in the number of bills which are being put on hold, particularly in Unit 3.

---

4 Recommendations

Finally, there should be a recommendation section. The recommendations should be based upon the findings of the report and this section should provide a forum for suggested changes in policies or a particular course of action, to improve collections or solve inherent problems.

> **An Example Recommendation:**
> Cash collection has continued on line but there is some scope for improvement. It is suggested that the credit controller particularly concentrate on the top 20% of bills (value wise) which hold 80% of the debt. A further effort is needs to reduce the number of bills in query and to speed up the time taken to deal with queries.

Summing Up The Usefulness Of Reports

The Credit Management/Debtor Report is the logical conclusion to a Credit Management System. It is the only method by which the Managing Body can monitor whether the Policies it has instigated are working or not. The Report should be simple and concise, easy to put together and easy to understand.

> ### *Achievements*
>
> Putting together a selection of Aged Debt Reports which will enable the practice to monitor its progress with regard to debtors.

Conclusion

Setting up an effective method for ensuring maximum profitability for the work it undertakes should be on the agenda for every forward thinking practice. The formulating of any credit policy with the aim of maximising profits needs to be based on the successful balance of the client's needs and the financial needs of the practice.

The debtors of a practice are usually the largest users of working capital. It is important for the profitability of the practice that working capital is never allowed to sit and stagnate in the debtors ledger, but rather that it be converted into cash as quickly as possible. The quicker the conversion takes place, the bigger the profit maintained, the higher the level of possible re-investment and distributions.

The three stages:

- Client Agreements
- Credit Control and
- Debtor Reporting

discussed in this book are intended to be inter-linked, and whilst it is possible just to have client agreements, or a credit control procedure, it most effective to use all the three elements together.

Effectiveness can be measured by an improvement in profits through reduced bank interest payments or improved cash reserves.

Index

Aged Debt 164–5, 175–6
Aged Debtors Reports 82–4

BACS 133
bankruptcy 29
billing 38
   in client agreements 13, 16
   and disbursements 40
   financial checklist 41
   telephone calls 47
   timing 39–40
billing targets 39, 73
bills 38–9
   formatting 42–4
   types 40–1
breakdowns 44–6

calendar system 84–5
cash flow projections 53
chasing procedures *see* collection procedures
client agreements 19, 193
   samples 20–2, 24
   working within 35
client files 34–6
client meetings 11–12
   agenda 12–18
   aims 18
   subsequent action 18–19
client-practice relationship 10–11, 25, 53
   and chasing procedures 73–4
   and credit controllers 119
   and telephone collection calls 70, 110, 111, 113
clients
   history logs 86–9
   risk assessment 29, 66

see also corporate clients; private clients
collection cycle 66, 68–74
   timing 71–2
collection procedures 68
   automatic systems 85
   calendar system 84–5
   checks and balances 72–3
   letters 68–71, 97–101
   options 96–7
   Procedures Manual 73–4
   record keeping 86–9
   statements 113–16
   telephone 68–71, 108–13
communication 72–3, 127–8, 133
Companies House 79
complaints 127
complaints procedures 13, 18
completion statements 44
confidentiality 43, 70–1, 109, 132
contracts *see* client agreements
conveyancing, billing 40
corporate clients 68, 69–70, 96, 97
costs
   breakdowns 44, 45
   estimates 13, 17
courtesy 127
credit agencies 79–80
credit checks 29, 76–7
   agencies 79–80
   ostrich condition 80
   simple and free 78–9
credit controllers 7, 58–9, 63, 118
   and fee earners 126–9
   selection 119–22
   training 122–6, 129–30
credit limits 30
   adhering to 77–8

setting 61
Credit Management 80, 129
Credit Management Policy 58–62
   and interdepartmental conflict 62–3
   presentation to staff 63
Credit Management Reports *see* Debtors Reports
Credit Management Systems 52
   administration 82–93
   collection techniques 96–116
   credit checks 76–80
   policy aim 52–3
   problem avoidance 131–3
   team work 6–8, 54
credit terms 17, 23
   setting 60–1
customer care *see* client-practice relationship

Daily Cash Collection Analysis 179–80
Data Protection Registrar 145
databases
   importance 144
   information 13, 18, 145–9
   starting off 144–5
   upkeep 150–2
debtor analyses 172, 174–80
Debtor Days Analysis 165–9, 172, 176
Debtor Reports 193
Debtor Status Analysis 177–8
debtors
   identifying 82–5
   importance 54
   Pareto principle 125
Debtors Reports 138, 154, 161–2, 164, 181
   Aged Debtors 164–5
   and cash flow projection 160–1
   conclusion and recommendations 180–1
   contents 156–8
   debtor analyses 165–9, 172–80
   fee earner attitudes 139
   feedback 160
   format 139–40
   frequency 154–5
   information flow 140–1
   presentation 159–60

   recipients 155–6
Direct Debits 105
disbursements 28
   billing 40, 41
   breakdowns 44, 46
   in client agreements 13, 16–17, 25
   exposure levels 61
   funding 61–2
   management 53
   record keeping 35
   Solicitors Accounts Rules 123
distress purchases 13

escalation techniques 100–1
expenses *see* disbursements
exposure levels *see* credit limits

fee boosters 73
fee earners 6–7
   and credit controllers 62, 126–9
   and Debtors Reports 139, 155, 160
   paying in receipts 124
fee levels 13, 15
final bills 40, 41
financial exposure, minimising 28–31
financial reports *see* Debtors Reports

graphs 164

history logs 86–90

Individual Voluntary Arrangements 29
insolvency 78–9
instalment payments
   arranging 125–6
   chasing letters 101, 105–6
   record keeping 87, 89
Institute of Credit Management 129–30
interim bills 16, 25, 40–1, 78–9
   and credit limits 30

Late Payment of Commercial Debts (Interest) Act 1998 23, 60
late payments 52, 54
   causes 167
   interest 23, 60
Legal Aid 15, 147
Legal Expenses Insurance 147
legal terminology 14, 122

letters
   as collection technique 68–71, 96, 97–101
   samples 102–7
Letters before Action 73, 101
   sample 104
limited companies, credit checks 79

no win, no fee agreements 16

ostrich condition 80
overheads 5

Pareto Principle 83, 125
part payment 107
paying in systems 124–5
payment promises logs 91–2
private clients
   collection techniques 68, 70–1, 96, 97–8
   credit checks 78, 79
problem avoidance 131–3
Procedures Manual 73–4

query logs 91–2

record keeping
   history logs 86–90
   query logs 91–2
   remittance advices 91
   telephone logs 113
remittance advices 91
reporting *see* Debtors Reports
reporting structure 59
risk assessment 29–30, 61, 66
   see also credit checks

seven day letter *see* Letters before Action
small businesses 23
Solicitor's Accounts Rules 1991 16–17, 122–3
staggered payments *see* instalment payments
stalling tactics 44, 52
Standing Orders 105
statements 96, 113–14
   contents 114, 116
   pros and cons 114
   sample 115
   timing 116

team work 54, 72–3, 118
telephone collection 68–71, 96, 97, 108
   delaying tactics and queries 110–13
   establishing relationships 110
   making the call 110
   preparation 108–9
   timing 109
   unavailable clients 113
third party bills 43, 98
   statements 114
time sheets 34–5
training 119
   courses 129–30
   credit controllers 122–6
   inter departmental 126–9

VAT 40, 43

work flow stages 6
Work in Progress (WIP) 61